CW00418195

RADICAL LEADERSHIP

RADICAL LEADERSHIP

In the New Testament and today

Michael Green

First published in Great Britain in 2017

Society for Promoting Christian Knowledge
36 Causton Street
London SW1P 4ST
www.spck.org.uk

Copyright © Michael Green 2017

All rights reserved. No part of this book may be reproduced or transmitted in any
form or by any means, electronic or mechanical, including photocopying, recording,
or by any information storage and retrieval system, without permission in writing
from the publisher.

SPCK does not necessarily endorse the individual views contained in its publications.

The author and publisher have made every effort to ensure that the external website
and email addresses included in this book are correct and up to date at the time of
going to press. The author and publisher are not responsible for the content, quality
or continuing accessibility of the sites.

Unless otherwise noted, Scripture quotations are taken from the HOLY BIBLE,
NEW INTERNATIONAL VERSION. Copyright © 1973, 1978, 1984 by International
Bible Society. Used by permission of Hodder & Stoughton Publishers, a member
of the Hachette UK Group. All rights reserved. 'NIV' is a registered trademark of
International Bible Society. UK trademark number 1448790.

British Library Cataloguing-in-Publication Data
A catalogue record for this book is available from the British Library

ISBN 978-0-281-07866-0
eBook ISBN 978-0-281-07867-7

Typeset by Fakenham Prepress Solutions, Fakenham, Norfolk NR21 8NN
Manufacture managed by Jellyfish
First printed in Great Britain by CPI
Subsequently digitally printed in Great Britain

eBook by Fakenham Prepress Solutions, Fakenham, Norfolk NR21 8NN

Produced on paper from sustainable forests

In honour of my friend Dr Lindsay Brown,
one of the wisest, most influential and most modest
leaders of his generation

Contents

Introduction

There are many excellent books on leadership in general, and a number on Christian leadership. I am not attempting to match their wealth of practical wisdom. But as a Christian I am concerned to commend the principles of leadership which we discern in the New Testament among Jesus and his close followers. Those leaders, though untrained in any seminary, turned the world upside down. So often our leaders, however many degrees they may have, do not.

Let me introduce you to the background of this book. I have been involved in the training of Anglican ordinands for much of my life, and I believe the training is rather similar in the theological institutions of most denominations. But I look back on it with some hesitancy. Let me outline a few of my concerns. I wonder: are we serving young men and women best when we take them as enthusiastic Christians away from the church where they worship and the jobs where they witness for Christ, and put them in an institution where they spend much of their time learning Greek and perhaps Hebrew, writing essays on Church history, ethics and doctrine, and living in an ecclesiastical bubble?

Our residential system certainly has some major advantages. They gain basic knowledge of the original languages, some deepened understanding of Christian doctrine, some awareness of the successes and failures of the Church down the ages, some insight into the increasingly complex ethical issues of the day. They gain from companionship with others who are heading for the same goal. And rough edges of character are often smoothed out by close contact with their peers.

All this is undeniably valuable, but the disadvantages need to be weighed. If they are married, students either live away from their spouse, or the family is uprooted to live in some small house near the college. While the ordinand is in training, the wife (it is usually a wife) either takes a job so as to keep bread on the table, or looks after young children and does not gain the opportunity for training in shared ministry with her husband. The programme is wasteful, being based on university terms which consist of three nine-week terms: this allows nearly half the year to be unused, so far as training goes – apart from a placement or two. Most colleges are dominated by determination to do university diplomas or degrees, rather than by the specific needs of ministerial training. As a result the student may be knowledgeable about the documentary hypothesis of the Pentateuch and the Form Criticism of the Gospels, but is unlikely to use any of this material at any time in his or her ministry. However, have the students been given any extended training in how to respond to an atheist or help an adult enquirer to Christ?

This concern of mine is not new. As long ago as 1877, the Revd Dr R. B. Girdlestone, head of translation at the British and Foreign Bible Society and the first principal of Wycliffe Hall, Oxford, wrote:

> Even if a man has passed an examination in such books as Aristotle's *Ethics* and Butler's *Analogy*, he may be utterly non-plussed when one whose heart the Lord has opened presses him earnestly with the question 'What must I do to be saved?' He may have written clever essays for his College Tutor and taken part in a debate in the Union, but may yet be totally unfit to minister to the sick and dying, to the ignorant and the stupid, to the indifferent and the hostile.

Did Girdlestone have a point?

The time spent by most ordinands in college does not include much in the way either of evangelism or of pastoral training; the latter is vitiated by being a short-lived affair of an hour or two a week that inevitably remains shallow because the student lives in the college, not the community. When the three (sometimes two) years are over, something of a lottery takes place. Experienced ministers in search of assistants send to the college a description of their work, and the student goes to see a likely one. It will only be for a weekend, or perhaps a second weekend when he takes his wife. The hope is that, based on this very frail encounter, a good relationship will emerge between the training leader and the trainee. Sometimes it does. But the casualties are many. And in any case the student has now suffered a double dislocation, first from his home setting to the college, and then from the college to a church where he may or may not fit. Is this really the best training we can give our ordinands?

I think the answer must be No. Look at the way in which other professionals are trained. Doctors spend some time in academic work but are soon learning on the job through clinical exposure and hospital rounds. Teachers are also speedily introduced as trainees to the classroom. But potential ministers have three years in a college which often renders them unable to meet the man in the street with a gospel which is good news to him. It is hardly surprising that in one Anglican diocese I visited recently 56 churches had congregations of less than 30 members. It is out of concern for this situation that the present book emerges.

I certainly do not want to belittle the excellent work done in so many theological colleges. And the Anglican training system has an enormous asset: after ordination it gives the student three years of practical experience of ministry under the eye of a seasoned vicar. This is a chance for young ministers to discover their gifts – and make mistakes without carrying final responsibility! The weakness of most non-Anglican denominations is that they, for reasons of finance or manpower shortage, tend to place the student in sole charge immediately after graduation. This of course has obvious dangers.

Despite the weaknesses, there are many good things in the current training offered in theological colleges. But I wonder if it could be supplemented. Here are some suggestions, drawn from other settings.

On a recent visit to Athens I was struck by the way the Bible College of Greece handled the problem. It was a remarkable institution of about 40 students. The faculty was of a high quality, most of them with doctorates. But they did not receive a salary. They gave their time, usually alongside parochial ministry, and some of them were financed as missionaries. But that set a model of sacrifice which was not lost on the students. The programme, too, was unusual. They worked and worshipped until 2 p.m., then all had a meal together, and then dispersed for practical ministry among the refugees and particular needs of the churches. That gave an excellent balance between academic input and pastoral output in their training.

When Yong Ping Chung was bishop in Sabah, East Malaysia, he went about it another way. He would not allow anyone to go to theological college who had not led someone else to faith. How could a pastor lead a church in evangelism, he reasoned, if he himself had never helped another individual into faith? And when the student had finished his academic training, Bishop Yong did not ordain him until he had demonstrated some practical usefulness as an assistant in one of the churches. As a result the quality of his clergy was very high.

In parts of Indonesia they will not allow you to train for full-time leadership until you have founded a small church. If that policy were followed in the West the number of ordinands would be radically reduced! But it certainly tends to produce leaders who are well trained for practical ministry.

Manfred Kohl, who has worked for 40 years with the Overseas Council, and (uniquely!) has visited every seminary and Bible college in the world, had a different recommendation. He, too, had come to the conclusion that theological institutions do not always do a great job in equipping students for ministry. He suggested that there were a number of important issues on which courses are rarely offered, but which a seminary should accommodate. They included:

Teaching on possessions – sharing and giving
Teaching on how to pray
Teaching on servant ministry
Teaching on management
Teaching on the kingdom of God.

It would not be difficult to add to this list – gender issues are increasingly clamant, yet we shy away from them. Islam is a major rival to Christianity, yet many theological institutions do not examine it in any depth. Apologetics is vital in a post-Christian Europe, yet this is totally neglected in many theological colleges. The trouble with adding topics like these is that there simply is not room in the timetable – unless there is a radical change in the amount of time the student spends at the college. And that would be very challenging to almost every denomination's training programme.

Various colleges have attempted to meet some of the concerns I voiced above, by means of mixed-mode and part-time training, thus allowing students to stay in their homes and workplace while training. This has quite a lot to be said for it, though it inevitably lowers academic standards. But one college, St Mellitus, has had the courage to make a radical break with the traditional system, and consequently it is hardly surprising that students are flooding to it: it has become by far the largest theological college in England. Founded in 2007, it has three centres – London, Chelmsford and Liverpool – with another planned for Plymouth. It is trans-denominational, operating with 'a generous orthodoxy', and offers a wide variety of courses. You can do full-time ordination training there – but half of the week must be on location in a church or mission context. You can do part-time ordination training, taking a longer time, but one which relates theological training to work, home, family, church and society. You can train as a youth worker. You can even start to study theology without any prior academic qualifications. This clear-sighted, radical and flexible way of training is surely the direction we must pursue for the future if we hope to see a revival of mature, integrated Christian leadership. This whole approach spells hope, and in the light of that hope I want in this book to examine the qualities Jesus and his apostles expected to see in the leaders they commissioned.

1

Jesus, the leader

'Smith is not a born leader – yet', exclaimed a despairing manager. But what could he or Smith do about it? Born leaders are in short supply. Indeed the whole idea of leadership is scorned in some intellectual circles: yet we can't do without it. In a world where problems are so great that it becomes impossible for any one person to handle them, where are we to look for healthy leadership?

It is interesting to notice the qualities which military leaders have considered important. The US Marine Corps rate integrity, knowledge, courage and decisiveness as the four most important characteristics of the good leader. The Royal Naval College, Dartmouth, prioritize faith, courage, loyalty and sense of duty. Field Marshal Lord Slim, who commanded the 14th Army in the Burma Campaign in the Second World War, chose courage, willpower, initiative and knowledge as his vital ingredients in a leader.

Courage, initiative, decisiveness and the rest – none of them are about technical performance. They penetrate much deeper to what people really are, to the moral and spiritual foundations of leadership. That has always been the hardest place to reach, and it is harder still in our postmodern society, with its particular beliefs. These include denial of absolutes and suspicion of truth claims; a personalized, relativistic morality replacing traditional moral values; distrust of authority and emphasis on choice. It includes cynicism about institutions, such as the law, monarchy, the Church and Parliament. It lives for the present and is both impatient of the past, and uncertain of the future. And yet there is a spiritual hunger in society as is evidenced by Eastern meditation, the New Age and our fascination with the occult. Top concerns today seem to be identity, meaning, purpose and relationships. It is not easy to exercise wise leadership in such a climate.

Perhaps three qualities emerge as vital for any leader in today's world. He or she must be willing to show initiative in formulating plans and ideas: leaders must lead. He must be able to set an example that will motivate others to follow. And he must care for those he seeks to lead, putting himself out for them, building relationships with them, because relationships are much more powerful than structures in eliciting enthusiasm and loyalty. In leadership, what we are is much more important than what we do. People will follow a leader who has won their love and respect. They may obey a hard taskmaster but they will never risk their lives for him.

So let us look a little deeper. As Leighton Ford acutely pointed out in *Transforming Leadership*, for many years discussions on leadership have centred on a transaction, an exchange. The leader gives the reward in exchange for the performance. But there is another kind of leader who transforms a situation – a John Wesley in religion, or a John Kennedy in politics.

Transactional leaders work within a situation.
Transformational leaders change it.
Transactional leaders accept what can be talked about.
Transformational leaders transcend it.
Transactional leaders accept the normal rules and values.
Transformational leaders change them.
Transactional leaders talk about payoff.
Transformational leaders set goals.

Of course this sort of leadership is a double-edged sword. Whereas Mother Teresa lifted the goals and aspirations of the Indian poor, Jim Jones led 900 followers in a downward spiral which ended in mass suicide. So where can we look for reliable examples of transformational leadership? Alexander the Great, who conquered the known world but died, apparently in a drunken orgy, at 33? Napoleon Bonaparte, the great commander who captured most of Europe, but ended up imprisoned in St Helena? John Kennedy, who exercised world power, but could not control his own sensuality? Where are we to look for an unblemished model of moral and spiritual leadership? The obvious answer is Jesus of Nazareth. Napoleon himself reflected that, 'If Charlemagne or Alexander the Great were to enter this room, we would all get up out of our chairs in respect. If Jesus Christ came in here we would all fall down on our faces in worship.' Jesus is unquestionably the greatest leader ever. More than two thousand years after his death a third of the human race professes allegiance to him. And yet this Jesus lived in a tiny village, had no home, never wrote a book or went to college, and died at 33. How can it be that he provides the greatest model for leadership? Here are some suggestions.

First, he knew who he was. That provided a solid core to his being. He knew he was God the Father's only Son, and he spent time with him. What he did in his ministry proceeded from who he was. He was not constantly tossed about by the vagaries of public opinion, the attacks of enemies or the adulation of friends. He exemplified the truth that what we are is much more important than what we do. If we are always wondering what people will think of us we cannot lead. Our true identity lies in our relationship with the God who created us, not in the tasks we perform and the status we achieve. We have all seen people so wrapped up in their work that they go to pieces when retirement strips them of it. If you are going to lead others, you have to be very sure who you are. Jesus was.

Second, he had a very clear vision. Karl Marx concluded his Communist Manifesto with the words 'You have a world to win.' He was right. Jesus had that same clarity of vision and subordinated everything to it. He had come to found an alternative society, the kingdom of God in the midst of the political kingdoms of the earth. Justice, integrity and community were among his goals, along with the greatest of them all – reconciliation with God. Mere managers want to do things right. Real leaders want to do the right thing, and they have the courage and vision to go for it. When Field Marshal Lord Slim took command of the 14th Army in Burma during the Second World War, he enunciated three principles which transformed the morale of the soldiers. First, there must be a great and noble aim. Second, it must be essential to achieve it. Third, every man must feel that what he is and does is important for achieving that goal. Jesus embodied that clarity of vision.

Third, his example was magnetic. People listened to him, watched him, followed him, laid down their lives for him, because his teaching was so self-evidently wonderful and because he genuinely practised what he preached. He taught 'Love your enemies . . . forgive your persecutors' – and he did precisely that. He taught that nobility consisted in service rather than being served – and he washed his disciples' feet. He taught that the greatest love anyone could have was to lay down his life for his friends – and then he eclipsed it by dying for his enemies. The point is clear. Unless people see leaders modelling what they teach, they will give them scant respect. Charisma without character is a catastrophe.

Fourth, he was servant of all, although he was the Lord of all. Throughout the gospel account we see him putting himself at the disposal of the multitudes, the poor, the lonely, the sick, the enquirers. Consistently he put himself last. Real leadership springs not from asking 'How many people will help me?' but 'How can I best serve others?' When that attitude is in place, people will follow a leader through hell and high water. A modern example is Queen Elizabeth II. When she came to the throne she vowed that her whole life, whether it be long or short, would be devoted to the service of her people. And 60 years later she is still carrying out that vow, working more than 40 hours a week on a staggering round of engagements. She observed 'God sent his only Son to serve, not to be served. He restored love and service to the centre of our lives in the person of Jesus Christ.' And, as Andrew Marr, the political commentator, points out, 'there are no reliable recorded incidents of the Queen losing her temper, using bad language, or refusing to carry out a duty expected of her'. No wonder the whole country was moved, and celebrated her 90th birthday with admiration and affection.

Fifth, he equipped and enabled his followers. Jesus refused the role of the manager behind the big desk, but chose, if anything, the image of the inverted cone. He concentrated first and foremost on three men in his inner circle. Then he poured himself into a group of 12, and then, to a lesser extent, 70 others. It was brilliant leadership. He did not dominate them, but enabled them to discover and use their own gifts. He utterly dedicated himself to those disciples, and yet he was ready to step aside and let them get on with it when they were ready. One of the great weaknesses of many leaders is that they have illusions of their own indispensability. Nobody could say that of Jesus, the supremely great leader and equipper of his followers.

Sixth, he was loyal to Scripture. As the ultimate embodiment of God's self-disclosure to mankind he might well have sat loose to the more shadowy adumbrations of God's purposes in the Old Testament. But no. He saw the Old Testament Scripture as the pattern and authority for his ministry, and he lived to fulfil it. He was far less influenced by tradition, political correctness and expediency than he was by the Scriptures. Time and again 'It is written' formed his clinching argument; and all his major initiatives, all his core teaching, all his self-understanding sprang from that source. That is not a notable feature among some of the Christian leaders I have known.

Seventh, he was radical and challenging. No other human being has ever given us such a radical appraisal of human nature, and such radical action for others. He knew that human nature itself was the critical battle ground. That is where the best-laid plans often collapse, because human nature has an endemic disease, sin, which Jesus unmasked. Human sin does not arise primarily from lack of education, poverty, psychological malfunction or from any external source. It comes from within human nature itself. Here was Jesus' analysis:

> Nothing outside a man can make him 'unclean' by going into him. Rather it is what comes out of a man that makes him 'unclean' . . . For from within, out of men's hearts, come evil thoughts, sexual immorality, theft, murder, adultery, greed, malice, deceit, lewdness, envy, slander, arrogance and folly. All these evils come from inside and make a man 'unclean'.
>
> (Mark 7.15, 21–23)

Can we deny it?

But Jesus did not merely recognize the extent of human sin. He bore the brunt of it on the cross. Field Marshal Montgomery once explained on a radio programme how this came home to him. He was a junior officer in the First World War and his platoon had been ordered to proceed across No Man's Land and attack the German lines. He gave strict instructions that if any man fell he was to be left there while the attack continued. He himself was shot to the ground, but one of his comrades disobeyed orders, picked him up and carried him back to the Allied trenches. As he heaved Montgomery into the trench the man was pulverized by machine gun fire and died. Monty remarked: 'Then I understood the cross of Christ.'

Jesus not only understood the nature of sin and bore its brunt, but he broke its power. Good Friday was followed by Easter. He had earlier declared 'everyone who sins is a slave to sin' but then went on to say 'So if the Son sets you free, you will be free indeed' (John 8.34, 36). His resurrection demonstrated that he had the power to deliver people from the grip of evil habits. The apostle Paul declares that the very power which raised Jesus from the dead is at work in the lives of believers to set them free (Eph. 1.19ff.). Time and again I have seen the truth of that, in people transformed by the power of the risen Jesus Christ. For example, I am in regular touch with a remarkably gifted evangelist among prisoners in North America. He was a very lost man when I had the joy of leading him to Christ years ago. In every letter, he tells me about conversions among the prisoners he visits. The other day he asked me to pray for Ron, a bright, intelligent man who had made a fortune in selling drugs. Ron listened, fascinated, to the story of Zacchaeus' conversion, and my friend continued:

> We went down on our knees together and he surrendered, just like I did with you 45 years ago this month! Christ is alive for sure! Ron has 10 more years to do in a federal penitentiary. He's going to be a strong witness in the jail. Glory be to God!

Such was the radical action Jesus undertook for us. But his challenge was no less direct. He dared to challenge the rich, the prostitutes, the demonized, the political and ecclesiastical leaders. He challenged people to exercise faith even in the most unpromising circumstances. He challenged people to reconsider their presuppositions and the priorities of their lives.

And when he challenged people 'Come, follow me', he expected them to respond. Many of them did.

Eighth, he was willing to sacrifice. That is essential in a great leader. It is costly to be unjustly attacked without hitting back, costly to bear pain rather than inflict it. It is costly to be so committed to the welfare of those you lead that you are prepared to suffer for them. He did just that, supremely on the cross which has ever since become the pre-eminent symbol of gallantry, symbolized by the Victoria Cross and the George Cross. Self-sacrifice like that has an enormous impact. Well might he say: 'The Son of Man did not come to be served, but to serve, and to give his life as a ransom for many' (Matt. 20.28). Leaders who, like Churchill and Garibaldi, offer their followers 'blood, toil, tears, and sweat' and are willing to endure it themselves – these are the leaders who change the world.

Finally, he was vulnerable. He was vulnerable to exhaustion, loneliness, criticism, betrayal, pain and a terrible death. When followers see us shed our fake masks of invulnerability and come over as the frail human beings that we are, albeit strengthened by God's grace, they will love us and respect us not less but more. That was true of the followers of Jesus. It is universally the case.

Whether consciously or unconsciously the outstanding leaders that I have met all exhibit most of these characteristics of Jesus Christ. They have tended to adopt these crucial characteristics of their Master's leadership. I would love to see these qualities more required of ordination candidates, but on the whole little training in leadership is offered in most theological institutions in the West. Students are trained to do things that churches normally do, but are not trained in the type of leadership exhibited by Jesus.

By contrast, that is often what you do find in young leaders in Africa and Asia. To be sure they are not perfect. Poverty makes corruption tempting and widespread. But on the whole, although they have so few resources and are usually operating in a hostile environment, they have a clear goal and are prepared to make great sacrifices to see it achieved. Perhaps that goal is geographical – reaching an urban block of flats with the gospel. Perhaps it is generational – a church run for and by teenagers. Perhaps it is reproductive – to double the congregation within a year. There is often a clear delineation of goals, then a wholehearted commitment to prayer, abundant love, vibrant human relationship, witness-bearing, conversion and nurture. The Christians in Africa and Asia seem to believe in growth before they see it. God honours faith and leadership of that quality. It is reminiscent of Jesus.

2

Jesus' training methods

In any organization, the training and equipping of colleagues is a primary requirement. Jesus certainly paid great attention to it. He came to announce the arrival of the kingdom of God, and if his cause was to have any future after his execution, the careful training of his mainly uneducated followers was essential. The same holds good today. Any leader worth his salt invests heavily in his followers so that the work can go ahead and flourish.

But when we look at the training common in Christian circles today, it appears to be radically different from the way Jesus went about it. Of course we cannot go directly from his practice in a tiny Middle Eastern country two thousand years ago to the present day, but since our training approaches are so vastly different from his own, we might be wise to see how the man who founded the Christian faith went about it.

Rabbis in Judea, like sophists in Greece, did much of their teaching as they walked around, surrounded by their followers. Their training was primarily practical, and theological issues were dealt with as they arose. Jesus was seen as a rabbi, and his training methods were those of a rabbi. There was no college or residential training, no lectures or exams, no book learning or essays. All these are regular features in the training of Christian clergy and pastors today. I fear our system often dulls the fire of students coming in to college. Within a few months their concern is not so much to reach people but to get good grades. There is a tendency for the programme to concentrate on academic rather than ministerial skills, and produce leaders who love books, research and higher degrees instead of the passionate desire to bring the gospel to people and be involved in their nurture. Then outcome of such training is less than encouraging.

It is time to see how Jesus went about training his future leaders.

Selection

In the first place *he selected them*. Though the accounts are sketchy in the gospels we can well imagine that Jesus spent some time with each of them during the early part of his ministry in Galilee. Otherwise it is unlikely that after a simple invitation 'Come, follow me', coming out of the blue, they would have responded with such alacrity. He had clearly got to know a wide variety of those who thronged around him, and we read that he spent a night in prayer before selecting his close band of 12, who would become representatives of the 12 tribes of the new Israel.

They were a very varied bunch. James and John were probably his cousins, their mother Salome being sister to the virgin Mary. It could have been objected that the dreamy John was far too young for such a calling: but Jesus chose him. At all events they were an impetuous pair, 'sons of thunder' as Jesus nicknamed them. Peter was a rough, headstrong, warm-hearted working fisherman. Simon was attracted to the Zealot movement, committed to removing the Romans by violence. He was the complete antithesis to Matthew, who farmed taxes for the hated Romans. Matthew was very much the customs official, skilled in reading people and writing bills. Thomas was the thoughtful, hard headed businessman, Judas the financial wizard. They were very varied. It would seem that they all, perhaps apart from Judas, came from the north of Galilee, and that none of them had been to the rabbinic schools, the equivalent of our university education. This might seem an unpromising group of men if you were seeking to advance the kingdom of God in a resistant world. But these were the men Jesus selected, presumably from among a large number of enthusiastic followers. Leaders need more than enthusiasm. Jesus called for them to respond in wholehearted and costly surrender to him and to his cause. It would mean leaving the tax booth behind, abandoning the fishing boats and the dagger of the Zealots. There would be no guarantee of accommodation, employment or financing. It would be very costly. Yet they came. All but one stayed the course. Most of them gave their lives for Jesus and his cause.

I have noticed, over the years, that ministerial candidates, at least in the West, have become increasingly concerned to expect comfortable conditions of service. Perhaps they assess their job prospects, the possibility of promotion, the income they hope to gain, the housing they are prepared to accept, rather more than they did 40 years ago. I am bound to ask myself, and to ask those who are current leaders in the church, if we would have left our security, our home and our job to follow a charismatic carpenter with a vision of the kingdom of God. Some would, and they are the people who win a big following these days: they set the bar high for themselves and others are prepared to jump it. They are willing to go wherever Jesus calls them. But I fear they are in the minority. I am so impressed by the young men and women training for ministry in Europe and Africa who face a future without any assurance of home or salary, and they do so with enthusiasm, because of their burning desire to serve Jesus Christ.

Fellowship and sending

The second notable feature in the training Jesus gave is that he called them first and foremost *to be with him and only then to go out and act as heralds of the kingdom* (Mark 3.14). If they were going to represent him, the top priority must be to spend time with him and discover his priorities, his prayer life, his lifestyle and approach to ministry. Intimacy with Jesus is a pre-condition for effectiveness in service.

Being themselves

They learnt to relax and be themselves. The gospels record their Sabbath afternoon walk through the cornfields, exercising the time-honoured right to pluck ears of corn, rub them in their hands, and after blowing away the chaff, eat them. Many a country boy even today does the same at times. It points to a delightfully relaxed, cheerful crowd of young men on the trail of adventure, rejoicing in each other and in their leader. These were not the pale-faced saints from stained-glass windows but normal, lively young men loving the liberation of their new way of life.

Facing opposition

But they also had to learn to face opposition without quailing. It was no small thing in that hyper-religious society to face the combined opposition of Pharisees, Sadducees and Herodians. The Pharisees stood for Israel against Rome but did so in a low-key and unprovocative manner, fearful of the consequences if they made any political gesture. Instead they concentrated on the minutiae of Jewish religious observance. The Sadducees seem not to have been too bothered about such things, but were extremely keen to retain their own position. They were mainly wealthy men from noble families, and they threw in their lot with Rome, many of them no doubt reluctantly. But these were the men who held the reins of such devolved power as Rome allowed them, and they were determined to hold on to it. The Herodians, on the other hand, were a Jewish party who favoured the corrupt dynasty of Herod Antipas, the puppet ruler of Galilee. This was formidable opposition, sometimes encountered separately, sometimes as a combined assault. Would-be leaders need to be able to stand tall. They need to withstand opposition even when it comes from more than one source, from the assumed culture of the day, or from those who should be their friends. That is how leaders grow in understanding and courage. That is what makes people listen to them. A classic modern example is Bishop Desmond Tutu, who in loyalty to Christ stood uncompromisingly for freedom in the face of the apartheid rulers of South Africa.

Discovering their inadequacy

Their training involved discovering how inadequate they were. That is a hard lesson for confident, outgoing 20-somethings. It is a hard lesson for mature and successful ministers who have a good deal of experience to rely on. But the truth of the matter is that 'without me you can do nothing'. Nothing at all that will count for the kingdom of God. It is essential to learn this lesson if we are to be any use to our Lord. And it is a tough lesson to learn. The apostle Paul certainly found himself forced to admit it by his mysterious thorn in the flesh. His prayer for its removal was not granted, 'but he [the Lord] said to me, "My grace is sufficient for you, for my power is made perfect in weakness." Therefore I will boast all the more gladly of my weaknesses, so that Christ's power may rest on me' (2 Cor. 12.6ff.). The disciples had not yet learnt that, and a graphic example of their inadequacy occurs in Mark 9. Jesus and his inner circle had gone up Mount Hermon where the transfiguration took place, and when they descended they found a distraught father berating the remaining disciples. He was obviously aware of the remarkable ministry of teaching, healing and exorcism which marked this new Jesus movement, and had come with his demonized son, seeking deliverance. They could not offer it. But Jesus succeeds where they failed, and in some exasperation they ask 'Why couldn't we drive it out?' – a question which reveals both the reality of demon possession and their inability to handle it. I wonder how many Christian leaders today are like the disciples, unable to deal with a ministry of deliverance? At all events Jesus tells them that prayer is the answer. It is only the power of God which can banish this dark spiritual influence wrecking a young life. And it is only by calling on that power and commanding the oppressive spirit to depart and never return that either then or now these demonic forces can be cast out. Some Christian thinkers are cessationist: that is to say, they maintain that the miraculous happenings recorded in the Scriptures died out after the apostolic age. But this flies in the face of evidence from Christian writers for the next 300 years: Justin, Irenaeus, Clement, Origen, Tertullian, Gregory and Augustine all insist that these gifts were present in their day. To be sure, it is fashionable in the West to pooh-pooh the idea of Satan and the influence his spiritual cohort forces can have on human life. But in Africa nobody laughs. The demonic is what keeps witch doctors in business, though their professed cures are worthless imitations of the freedom that ministry in the power of Jesus can bring. Of course, this is only one example of unacknowledged inadequacy. There are plenty more!

Prayer

Prayer was something Jesus went out of his way to inculcate in his would-be leaders. He did so by his own repeated example which Luke in his Gospel is keen to emphasize. But he did so in particular when his disciples asked for help in prayer. He gave them what we call the Lord's Prayer, but in reality it is the prayer for disciples to use. It begins with the intimate family name for a father, in his native Aramaic tongue, *Abba*, Daddy. That is how we are to address the heavenly Father – not just *the* Father but *our* Father corporately. It continues with prayer for God's kingly rule to advance as lives of men and women surrender to the King. It asks for his will to run in the earthly realm as it does in the heavenly. Only then does it turn to petition for our needs. 'Give us each day our daily bread' may be a request for physical sustenance. But the unusual word *epiousios* can equally yield the translation 'Give us today the bread of tomorrow – sustain us with a foretaste of the life of the age to come'. In the light of Calvary we can confidently pray 'Forgive us our sins' but unless we are willing to offer similar forgiveness to others we erect a wall of refusal against God's pardon of ourselves. 'Do not bring us to the test', reflects our cry to God as we anticipate any testing circumstances in our lives and particularly the test of standing firm in the face of death or apostasy. 'Deliver us from evil', or, as it could equally be translated, from 'the Evil One', betrays a lively awareness of the spiritual battle and the need to cry to God for deliverance from a force too strong for us. I love the ascription at the end, perhaps a later addition or maybe given by Jesus on another occasion: 'for yours is the kingdom and the power and the glory for ever'. If our attitude is 'Yours is the kingly rule in my life today' we can be confident that God will give us the power to live that way, and we must then give all the glory, any credit that accrues, back to him, where it belongs.

That matchless short prayer, capable of being recited briefly as a whole or serving as a series of signposts for more extended prayer, must have amazed and thrilled his followers, accustomed as they were to much formality and often ostentation in the lengthy prayers of their culture. On any showing, prayer is a crucial lesson for all leaders to learn. Here again my fear is that in the West we have a very long way to go. We depend on our technology, our PowerPoint, our eloquence and our smartphones to achieve the results we desire. In the majority world where they have few of these advantages, they are driven to prayer, prayer alone, as the great way to discover and deliver what God desires. And it is in those parts of the world that the gospel is growing exponentially. Who would have guessed that the repressed Church in China should, in the few decades since Mao Zedong died, have grown to over a hundred million? Most of these Christians had no Bible, were allowed no build-ings, and their ministers were banished to labour camps. They depended on prayer alone. But how magnificently they grew!

Spiritual power

Spiritual power was another lesson they learnt in company with Jesus. One of the most amazing examples is found in the very first chapter of Mark's Gospel. Jesus' synagogue teaching was interrupted by a man who was demonized. He cried out: 'What do you want with us, Jesus of Nazareth? Have you come to destroy us? I know who you are, the Holy One of God.' Jesus was not going to welcome recognition from demons, and at once rebuked it saying: 'Be quiet . . . Come out of him!' And the unclean spirit, throwing him into convulsions and screeching with a loud voice, came out of him. They were all amazed, and they kept on asking one another: ' "What is this? A new teaching – and with authority! He even gives orders to evil spirits and they obey him." News about him spread quickly over the whole region of Galilee' (Mark.1.24ff). I bet it did! I remember the first time I encountered demonic interference. It was in Ghana in the midst of an evangelistic outreach. I sat next to a large Ghanaian student on a truckle bed and led her in a prayer of commitment to Christ. At once the atmosphere grew cold and she slumped senseless on to the bed. Not knowing what to do I simply cried out 'Jesus, Jesus' and she quickly recovered and began to rejoice in her new relationship with Christ. I met her, now a flourishing Christian, years later in New York! There have been many more dramatic cases since then, but this first experience is one I will not easily forget. When the first disciples saw things like this happening through the ministry of Jesus it must have amazed them just as this experience amazed me.

Healing

A lesson in deliverance ministry is closely followed by one in healing. Mark 2.1–12 shows not only the crowds besieging the house where Jesus was teaching, but the opposition in the shape of the scribes (closely allied to the Pharisees) who had come to check him out. Then comes the intriguing story of four men who were carrying a paralysed friend. They could not force their way in through the crowd, so they climbed the outside stairs, common in Eastern houses, and made a hole in the (presumably mud and brushwood) roof through which they let their friend down in front of Jesus. Magnificent improvisation! His disciples must have been surprised: the man's obvious need was healing, but Jesus told him: 'Son, your sins are forgiven.' That was enough to enrage the scribes. After all, who can forgive sins but God? Blasphemy! But Jesus said: ' "Why are you thinking these things? Which is easier: to say to the paralytic, "Your sins are forgiven," or to say, "Get up, take your mat, and walk?" But that you may know that the Son of Man [his favourite, and deliberately enigmatic, name for himself] has authority on earth [just as the Father has in heaven] to forgive sins, . . ." He said to the paralytic, "I tell you, get up, take your mat and go home." "Stand up, take up your mat and go home." He got up, took his mat and walked out in full view of them all. This amazed everyone and they praised God, saying, 'We have never seen anything like this!' That healing was a crucial part of the education of the Twelve. They came to recognize the sheer God-given authority both of the teaching and of the actions of Jesus. They had seen his power first in deliverance and then in healing.

Once again, I fancy that most students in theological seminaries have never seen anything like this. And yet the humblest believers in many parts of the world have. I recall an occasion in Malawi when I was speaking to a group of clergy. One of them had an injured leg and was unable to walk. After the meeting he asked for prayer. I felt diffident, but some of his colleagues had more faith than I did. They speedily crowded round and we laid hands on the leg and prayed earnestly for the man's healing. It was instantaneous! He jumped up and started walking, almost dancing around. I said, 'You will have something to say when you preach on Sunday.' 'I certainly will', was his reply. Humble African believers have often seen healing in the name of Jesus in answer to prayer, and they have been delivered from dark forces afflicting their lives when these have been commanded to depart in the name of Jesus. Of course we cannot organize such divine interventions. In our broken world prayer does not always bring the result we long for. But if we have never seen God's power released in healing or deliverance it is likely that we will become timid leaders, unlikely to expect great things from God or attempt great things for God.

Compassion for the needy

As they accompanied their Master, the Twelve would have seen him in various moods. Exultant when they achieved something in his name, patient in teaching the crowds, angry at blatant unbelief, but most of all full of compassion for those in need.

This is mentioned many times in the gospels, but perhaps the most moving is recorded in Matthew 9.35ff just after Jesus had cured two blind men. He was 'preaching the good news of the kingdom and healing every disease and sickness. When he saw the crowds, he had compassion on them, because they were harassed and helpless, like sheep without a shepherd. Then he said to his disciples, "The harvest is plentiful but the workers are few. Ask the Lord of the harvest, therefore, to send out workers into his harvest field." ' They did ask, and to their utter surprise they found that he sent *them*! They had been with him continuously. They had learned so much. Now they were ready to at least begin to move out in service.

Slow learning

The gospels go out of their way to stress that the disciples were slow learners. Repeatedly we are told that they did not understand. Three times at least Jesus told them, during the latter part of his ministry, that he would go up to Jerusalem, be arrested and handed over to the Romans by the Jewish hierarchy, and would suffer, be killed and rise again. Perhaps not surprisingly, they did not understand. This did not stop Jesus loving them, continuing to teach them, and trusting them. Those 12 were to represent the leadership of the new Israel, and he was determined to hold on to them, help them, teach them until they could stand tall and continue the work after he was gone. What a wonderful way to treat failures and slow learners! Tom Watson, founder of the corporate giant IBM, once asked a young executive to carry out a very risky venture. Ten million dollars were spent on the project which turned out to be a disaster. The young man offered his resignation. 'Resignation?' said Watson. 'You can't be serious. We've just spent ten million dollars educating you.' That was the attitude of Jesus to his very fallible followers.

Sharing in ministry

The third stage in their training was this. *He gave them a small share in the ministry.* He did not abruptly put them in charge, as some modern churches do, knowing that would be unwise. He simply allowed them to be participants in an enterprise where he was the main player. It must have been fascinating for them that 'Jesus travelled about from one town and village to another, proclaiming the good news of the kingdom of God. The Twelve were with him, and also some women' (Luke 8.1ff.). We are not told that they played an active role, but they were part of the big picture, learning as they watched Jesus in action. That is a great way to begin, as observers of someone more experienced. They do a little more as the Passion draws near. Jesus sends some of them ahead of him as he climbs the crest of the Mount of Olives. They are to go and find a donkey for his triumphal entry into the capital. He told them precisely where to find it, 'as you enter it [the village]' (Luke 19.29). He told them it was tied up, so they would have no difficulty in recognizing the animal. And he even told them what to say if challenged. The instructions were crystal clear, something of vital importance when young disciples are taking first steps in leadership. Again, he instructs two of his disciples to go into the city and look for the unusual sight of a man carrying a water-pot – unusual, for this was women's work. They are to follow him, and in the large upper room which he will show them, they are to make preparation for the Passover feast which Jesus will eat with his companions before his arrest and death. Again the very clear instructions. Again the small part in a big picture.

They had rather more to do during the two great feedings of multitudes, recorded in Mark's Gospel. In the feeding of the five thousand they come up with their own idea, pointing out to Jesus that it is late in the day, and that he should dismiss the crowds so that they could forage for something to eat in the villages. Jesus astounds them by saying 'You give them something to eat.' Their amazement and financial caution, born of poverty, surfaces: 'That would take eight months of a man's wages. Are we to go and spend that much on bread and give it to them to eat?' Jesus stretches their faith, understanding and compliance a bit further: 'How many loaves do you have? . . . Go and see.'

In his account John tells how Andrew and Philip found a lad whose lunch basket consisted of five loaves and two fish – 'but how far will they go among so many?' Doubt, lack of faith, perplexity – they all mingle with obedience. Jesus then gets them to organize the crowd and make them sit down in orderly groups on the green grass, green for only a couple of weeks in the spring. Jesus blesses the provisions and sees them multiply under his hand. The disciples hand the bread and fish around until everyone has had not just a bite but a satisfying meal. Then they are told to pick up what had dropped to the ground, and to their amazement they collected 12 baskets full of broken pieces of bread and fish. Mark takes valuable space in his short Gospel to tell of another occasion, this time not on Jewish but Gentile soil in Transjordan, where Jesus feeds four thousand from seven loaves and a few small fish. Again the disciples are racking their brains: where in that deserted place could anyone get enough bread to feed this tired and hungry crowd? Again Jesus stretches their faith and cooperation by getting them to find out what provisions they actually had with them – it turned out to be seven loaves and a few small fish. Again Jesus uses the Twelve to distribute the miraculously enlarged provisions. Again they are told to pick up the remains, in this case seven baskets full. Two things then happen in Mark's account which are very common as disciples launch out in ministry. First, there is the opposition of the Pharisees who, blind to what has just happened, asked for a sign from heaven! And second, they were worried about their own hunger during a boat crossing of the lake, for they had forgotten to bring bread. Jesus has to remind them of what they had seen his own power achieve in the two feedings. He concludes 'Do you still not see or understand?' They had been given a piece of the action, but their performance was marred by lack of understanding, doubt, forgetfulness, and probably fear of the critical eyes of the Pharisees upon them. These are all factors which tend to hamstring early efforts in Christian leadership.

Sent out by themselves

The fourth step in Jesus' training programme is to send his disciples away on a mission without him. He clearly rated the short intensive mission highly. In Luke 8.1 we find him engaged in an outreach of this sort with his disciples accompanying him. In Luke 9.1 we find him sending out the disciples on a similar mission without him. And in Luke 10.1 we find him doing the same with 70 (or as some manuscripts have it, 72) of his followers. These evangelistic and healing missions are all the more remarkable because they occur in the context of Jesus' final long journey when he 'resolutely set out for Jerusalem' (9.51) with the spectre of the cross before his eyes. Even at such a forbidding time, he regarded these missions as a critical element in the unfolding of the kingdom which he had come to usher in. The missions were certainly critical for his followers. This is where they came alive! The longest account is of the mission of the 70 in Luke 10. Many of the features in this account can be seen in similar mission outreaches today: not only are they effective, but they offer training that could never be gained in the classroom of a college. The current explosion of Christianity in China is due to a considerable extent to courageous, costly short-term mission by lay Christians who are passionate for Jesus.

Partnership

First, the disciples have to learn partnership if they are to be effective in mission. They go out two by two. There is little place for the lone ranger in Christian mission: partnership with others is far more satisfactory. It teaches interdependence. It offers encouragement. This remains a lesson Christians are slow to learn. There are too many prima donnas in evangelism. I often lead short-term missions with a small team in a university. But I invariably ensure that another evangelist shares the leadership with me. It can be lonely work, and the partnership of an experienced colleague is an enormous help and encouragement.

Attitude

Second, their attitude is very important. They are to recognize that they are a tiny minority battling against the prevailing attitude of society. The harvest may be plentiful (the fruit of that harvest will only appear later, when their work is assessed) but the labourers are certainly few. The way to surmount this problem is not by frantic activity but by begging the Lord of the harvest to send out workers. Thank goodness there is a Lord of the harvest, and it is not you or me! They are to go out on what will be a costly enterprise and probably a dangerous one. They go like lambs among wolves. And they are to go very simply, 'with no purse or bag or sandals' but with entire dependence on God, and with such a singleness of purpose that they hardly greet anyone on the way. In the West, these injunctions are rarely carried out. But here is an attractive exception. The Revd Dan Cozens has spent much of his life organizing and engaging in missions of this sort. He calls them 'The Walk of 1,000 Men' because of the large number of men who have at one time or another taken part. There is a clear itinerary: it might be around Cornwall, or along the border in Ireland. The team would go on a long hike, lasting a couple of weeks or more, stopping at the pubs and sleeping on the church floors. Each team member would only take enough money to buy someone a drink in the pub, and they would rely for food on the homes which welcomed them. They would chat to individuals about Christ, speak at small meetings, and pray for the people. I have been on one of these missions and it is a fascinating learning experience. I have no doubt it was for the 70!

Message

Their message was one of wholeness: 'Peace (shalom) be to this house.' The word indicates life at its best, wholeness. They are to be concerned for the whole person, not just the spiritual aspect. That peace might include prayer for healing, practical service, bringing reconciliation. At its best the Church has always been concerned to bring wholeness. But there must be a note of challenge in their mission. They come as messengers of the kingdom of God. If that message is received peace will flow. If it is rejected they are to shake off the dust of the place from their feet. 'The kingdom of God is near' and that kingly rule of Jesus demands decision, for him or against him. The contemporary Church in the West is either so obsessed with cultural and social aspects of life that there is little challenge; or else it is careless of physical needs but militant in challenging people who have little understanding of its message. Concern for wholeness and challenge need to combine in any balanced Christian mission.

Report back

Finally we note that the 70 returned with joy to report back to Jesus. It was a time of great joy. They told him about the exciting results of their ministry. Jesus saw this as clear evidence that Satan is a defeated foe and encouraged them to rejoice instead that they belonged to the winning side, the kingdom of heaven. But joy was paramount, and so was praise to the Father because through the witness of these amateur missionaries divine truth had been revealed to some of those who heard. I can echo that sentiment. I have been involved in many short missions, some in cities but most in universities in the UK and Europe. Always there has been partnership. Always risk. Never has there been payment. Always you don't quite know where the next meal is coming from. Always there is interest, always opposition, and always there are those who entrust themselves to Christ. On a single evening recently after a challenging address, five students made a profession of faith: they hailed from Mexico, the USA, Singapore, the UK and Italy. The kingdom of God had indeed come to them, and there was great rejoicing in the team coupled with praise to God. It was moving at the prayer meeting on the final morning of that mission to hear voices from all over the packed room raised to God in gratitude for what he was doing in the lives of their friends. Short evangelistic missions are indeed a marvellous way not only to reach others but to develop those who go on them.

Trusted leaders

Eventually Jesus judged the time was ripe to entrust the work to his new leaders. Mark's Gospel is cut short after 16.8 for reasons that are debated, but the other gospels all bear testimony to this commissioning of Jesus' close disciples before his Ascension. John records Jesus breathing on his disciples and saying 'Receive the Holy Spirit. If you forgive anyone his sins, they are forgiven; if you do not forgive them, they are not forgiven.' This is followed by chapter 21, the great call for the Church to 'catch fish' and 'feed sheep' until Jesus' returns. In Matthew's Gospel Jesus gives the Great Commission to his leaders (even though some were still plagued with doubts) to go and make disciples of all nations, confident in the power and the continued presence of their Lord. Perhaps the most significant is Luke's account. After opening their minds to understand the Scriptures more fully about his person, death and resurrection, Jesus predicts that they will proclaim 'repentance and forgiveness of sins in his name to all nations, beginning in Jerusalem'. Luke's second volume, the Acts of the Apostles, shows how courageously and innovatively that commission was carried forward.

How important it is for senior leaders to follow their Master's example and be prepared to relinquish control, to step out of the limelight, and to allow those they have trained to carry the torch. Only today I was hearing of a vicar who appointed a colleague with a view to planting a new church. But he could not bear to relinquish control, and determined, instead of trusting a colleague to run the church plant, to make it a satellite congregation instead, with himself as the ultimate controller of both. It is sad to see many promising gospel ministries set back a long way by the refusal of the leader to move aside. He can still be of use encouraging and advising, but the execution of the gospel mandate needs to be transferred to younger hands. That is what Jesus did. After careful training, Jesus entrusted the whole enterprise to them. He took the risk that they might fail. He believed they would succeed. And his judgement was magnificently vindicated. It was this odd bunch of Middle Eastern youngsters who changed the world.

3

Peter on leadership

The apostle Peter had a great deal to unlearn. He had been boastful, impulsive, almost truculent in his association with the other disciples during the ministry of Jesus. He had claimed he would die for Jesus rather than let him down. But when it came to the arrest, he first of all made a fruitless swish with his sword and cut off a man's ear, and then kept his head down, followed the soldiers back to the high priest's house at a distance, and three times denied that he even knew Jesus when he was accused of being his follower. His bombast was smashed, and his self-appointed leadership lay in shreds.

But mercifully that was not the end of the story. Jesus had foretold his denials, and had also predicted that when he came to repentance he would strengthen his brethren. Well, that process began when Jesus caught his eye in the high priest's courtyard. Utterly ashamed and unable to live with what he had done, Peter flung himself out and wept bitterly. The process of restoration moved on to a different level when the risen Jesus made a fire on the beach and provided breakfast for his disheartened followers who had gone back to fishing. After breakfast Jesus had taken Peter aside. Three times he asked him if he loved him. Three times a chastened Peter replied with a weaker word but trusted that Jesus knew his heart. And the very fallible Peter was recommissioned to 'tend Christ's sheep'.

Well, it is now 30 years later. Peter's experience of leadership had been transformed. The gospel had spread widely in those 30 years, as the book of Acts reveals. It reached Rome very early, since there were proselytes from Rome present at Pentecost, when all the believers were filled with the Holy Spirit of Jesus. The Church had expanded a lot in the capital during those 30 years – so much so that when the Great Fire burnt down a large part of the city in AD 64 the emperor Nero, accused of starting the fire himself in order to enlarge his palace gardens, cast the blame on the Christians. They must have been numerous by that time in order to provide even the sketchiest justification for such a claim. The Roman historian Tacitus tells us that a great multitude were arrested. 'Some were covered with the skins of wild animals and torn apart by fierce dogs, some were crucified, and others set alight and used for illumination when darkness fell' (Tacitus, *Annals* 15.44). It is possible that Peter refers to this outrage in 4.12ff of his first letter. He urges his recipients in Rome:

> Dear friends, do not be surprised at the painful trial you are suf-
> fering, as though something strange were happening to you . . .
> if you suffer as a Christian do not be ashamed, but praise God
> that you bear that name . . . those who suffer according to God's
> mill should commit themselves to their faithful Creator . . .

What a time for nerves of steel! What a time for true leader-ship. That is the subject Peter addresses in 1 Peter 5.1–11. What he has to say is as relevant to our day as it was to his. Moreover, it touches us all at some point because we all give the lead in some area or other, perhaps as a mother in the family, a boy or girl at school, a good athlete in a sports team or a busi-ness person in a lawyer's office, in finance, development or management.

There are seven aspects of leadership which Peter examines in these verses. He shows the difference it makes if we are hand-ling that leadership role as Christians.

Staff relationships

How is the leader to relate to his colleagues? Verse 1 is highly significant. There is no pride left in Peter by now, no sense of status. He is an apostle of Jesus Christ, no less. He is the rock on which Jesus would build his Church. But amazingly he simply calls himself a 'fellow elder'. Peter had come to believe in a team leadership, no longer in the one-man band. So he set himself on precisely the same level as the presbyters leading the Roman Church. That is eloquent, and a magnificent example for anyone placed in authority. There was an outstanding example of it in Greek history which, perhaps unwittingly, Peter followed. Alexander the Great, who captured almost the whole known world, believed in exactly the same principle. He dressed like an ordinary soldier, he ate with the men, and was in the front line of battle with them. As a result they adored him and would do anything for him. That is true leadership. If you want to lead, build a team: don't try to do all the leading yourself. And do not give yourself airs. Peter had learnt that lesson, so crucial for Christian leadership.

Leadership style

What Peter advocates is 'shepherding'. Not for Peter the large office of the managing director. Not for him the barked order from the general that brooks no denial. His model for leadership is that of a shepherd. A shepherd cares for his sheep, protects them, feeds them. Where did Peter get that idea about leadership from? Of course it was from the Chief Shepherd (v. 4) who had looked after him so patiently for three years and had commissioned him to feed sheep. This speaks of a servant leadership, an enabling leadership. That is the style proper for

Christian leadership. Our daughter Sarah is a shepherd as well as a vet. The sheep look to her for food every day – she has only to rattle the food bucket and they come running. But she is always on the lookout for sheep that fall over and can't get up, always blocking holes in the hedge. She is vigilant in inspecting them for footrot, regular in dipping and vaccinating them, quick to inject them with antibiotic if they unwell. At lambing time she is prepared to be up and in attendance all night long in order to assist in a difficult birth. That is the shepherd style enjoined on the Christian leader. It is a caring role, enabling, healing, life-giving. It did not come naturally to Peter, but at last he had learned it.

Motivation

Peter turns to this issue in verses 2 and 3. What fires the leader to work hard and put in long hours? What is the hidden spring coiled inside him or her? Well, it is not duty: 'not because you must', though duty can take us a short distance along the path of leadership. It is not money either: 'not greedy for money', a motive that has caused the downfall of countless leaders. Nor is it to gain self-satisfaction: 'not lording it over those entrusted to you'. The desire to exercise power, the lust for money, and the cold pull of duty – they characterize a lot of leadership today, as they must have done in Peter's day. But Peter will have none of it. The spell of Jesus' love and shepherding has never left him since his recommissioning. So he encourages them to offer leadership 'not because you must, but because you are willing to' – in gratitude for all their Lord has done for them. 'Not greedy for money but eager to serve', just as Jesus did not come to be served but to serve, and in the end give his life as a ransom for many. And their leadership should not be because they like ordering others around but because they are happy just to give an example. Those are the motives that inspire the true leader.

Lifestyle

There is a tendency in modern government, and not only there, to say 'We do not mind what you do in your discretionary time. We are interested in your doing your job properly. If your spare time activities prove a hindrance to your work you may be dismissed. But otherwise you are free to do what you want.' I remember when Tony Blair came to power in the UK he told his cabinet that nobody would be sacked for fornication or marital infidelity so long as their work in government was not affected. The trouble with this attitude is that what we do in our leisure time shows what we really enjoy and what we really are like. That is a character matter, and it is sure to show in our professional life, sooner or later. Hence the very public scandals involving money, sex and lies which come to light with depressing regularity whatever party is in power. What we are speaks more loudly than what we do. We are called to be examples. We have to put our life where our mouth is. We must walk the talk. This is very demanding but it is an essential element in leadership, particularly Christian leadership. It is no good saying to our children 'Now say your prayers before bed' if they know that we never pray. It is no good saying 'You must never tell a lie' when they can say 'But, dad, I heard you tell mum a great big whopper of a lie only yesterday.' Example is a crucial part of leadership.

Attitude

Success will sometimes come our way. How will we handle it? How will we behave towards colleagues who, perhaps, have had no such success in their area of ministry? Peter is very clear (verse 5). 'Clothe yourselves with humility towards one another, because [and here he quotes Prov. 3.34] 'God opposes the proud but gives grace to the humble.' The word he uses for 'clothe yourselves' is unique in the New Testament but it carries overtones of when Jesus girded himself with a towel and washed the feet of his disciples. That is how we are to react to success. Take the towel and see if we can wash the feet of our colleagues.

Peter gives two reasons for this remarkable advice. Pride is the primal sin which caused Satan to fall from angel to devil: 'God opposes the proud'. And the other reason is that God loves to give his strength to those who admit to him that they have none of their own: he 'gives grace to the humble'. Humility, a word twice repeated in this verse, is seen as a weakness in Aristotle, but it is a prime virtue among Christians, because it shines the spotlight away from ourselves and on to the one who gives us success. Moses was a great leader, and yet we read that he was the most humble man before God to be found anywhere on earth.

Humility does not mean running yourself down – and pretending you are no good. That would be to denigrate the gifts God has endowed you with. No, it means self-forgetfulness in your relationships with others and remembering how small you are before God. Humble leaders are usually great leaders. I had the privilege of being supervised in New Testament studies at Cambridge by the Lady Margaret Professor, C. F. D. Moule. Everyone who knew him was deeply impressed by his humility, yet at that time he was the leading New Testament scholar in the country. That is such an attractive quality, and accounts for the large number of ex-pupils the world over who loved and honoured him.

Anxiety

There is a very lonely aspect to leadership, however collegial we strive to be. Someone has to take the hard decisions. And the decisions that are problematic for others find their way to the desk of the main leader. All leaders therefore face anxiety at times. It goes with the uncertainty of life and the pressure of leadership. How should we handle it? Well, we should not handle it in the way the army colonel under whom I served did. He had a notice hanging up in his office: 'Don't worry. It may never happen.' Well it did happen! I was assistant adjutant and in charge during the absence of the colonel and adjutant. It was reported to me that a rifle had gone missing. My somewhat relaxed response was that in due course it would doubtless come to light. I mentioned this to the colonel on his return and he went pale and then almost wept, howling 'I shall lose my command!' He ordered a full search of the whole camp to be instituted, and the soldier who had it stashed away somewhere made haste to return it anonymously. That was an object lesson to me on how not to handle anxiety. Peter, in verse 7, has a much better plan: 'Cast all your anxiety on him', he says. Christ's back is broad enough to carry all our worries and he will, because literally 'it matters to him about you'. I have never seen that translation in any English version, but it is the delightful and immensely encouraging precise translation of the Greek. It matters to him about us, and he cares about the issue that is worrying us far more than we do. Our part is to cast the burden firmly and intentionally on Jesus.

Hard times

All leaders face hard situations at times. They may come from internal stress, external opposition, difficult circumstances, awkward people or some unexpected disaster. How are we to react to such times? Some leaders are driven to drink. Some panic and fall apart. Some blame subordinates. No, says Peter: 'Be self-controlled and alert.' Maintain your spiritual disciplines. Don't let hard times make you abandon them. Recognize that there is an anti-God force, the devil, who delights to manipulate the assaults that come our way. It is not enough to pray for his defeat. 'Resist him, standing firm in the faith.' Tell him to get lost! Know that your problems are not unique. Similar hardships are happening to brothers and sisters in Christ all over the world, and in many cases their situation is far graver than ours. Suffering is painful but it toughens our spiritual stamina. And 'the God of all grace . . . will make you strong, firm and steadfast'. He has the power, and it will last for ever!

This is fascinating, invaluable advice on Christian leadership from a man who had had to learn the hard way. It covers our relationships, our style of leadership, our motives, our behaviour, our attitude, our handling of money and setbacks. There are many personal touches in these verses. The shepherd imagery is explicitly drawn from Jesus the good shepherd. Likewise the emphasis on example comes from one who could credibly claim 'I have given you an example.' 'Clothe yourselves' is a vivid reminder of Jesus taking a towel, girding himself with it and washing the feet of his disciples. 'Make you strong' takes us back to Jesus' prediction at the Last Supper that Peter would deny him: 'when you have turned back, strengthen then your brothers' (Luke 22.32).

Yes, there are many personal touches in this chapter, but what these verses bring before us above all else is the note of transformation in Peter. What a changed man! Look at those seven marks of a Christian leader again, and note how far he had progressed.

- In team relations, he had once been bombastic, always keen to give his opinion, always wanting the number-one spot. Now, he modestly comes alongside his fellow elders.
- In leadership style, he had not cared overmuch about others. Now, shepherding is his model.
- In motivation, he had acted on impulse. Now, his motivation is gratitude.
- In lifestyle, he had been disastrous. Now, he is concerned to give a good example.
- In attitude, there had been no sniff of humility about him in the old days. Now, he is happy to don the towel of the servant.
- In anxiety, he had forgotten Jesus' injunction 'Let not your heart be troubled'. He had lost his cool and slashed out with his sword. Now, he is learning to cast his burdens on the Lord.
- In hard times, he had fallen asleep and run away when Jesus most needed his support because the arrest was imminent. Now, he is deeply concerned for the hardships his readers are undergoing.

What a change! But Peter had been a witness, among others, of the crucifixion of Jesus to take responsibility for his sins. And he had shared in the anticipation of future glory in the resurrection. Forgiven through the cross and empowered through the resurrection, he was a new man. I find this enormously encouraging. The Lord who changed Peter can work a similar change in any of us if we will let him. He can restore us as he restored Peter. He will make us strong and steadfast, qualities that are so needed in leadership. He is the God of all grace. He has called us to glory. His is the power for ever and ever. That power can make us God's leaders in the circles in which he has placed us. Allelulia!

4

Leadership at Corinth

Leadership is vital to any church, if only because a congregation rarely rises beyond the level of its leaders. Leaders at Corinth created a lot of problems. This can unfortunately still happen. Sometimes there is little vision, little actual leadership at all; instead, an abrogation of responsibility. Sometimes there is an attempt to impose the old monarchical pattern of leadership. Sometimes division is the order of the day, as rival factions tear the fellowship apart. Sometimes the magic word 'democracy' is uttered, committees proliferate, and little is done. What has the Corinthian correspondence to say about leadership?

It certainly knows all about the difficulties. The emergence of warring factions, each advocating their own candidates for leadership, was the main problem which caused Paul to write 1 Corinthians. There was massive immorality, wrangling about spiritual gifts and scepticism about the physical resurrection of Jesus. As 2 Corinthians makes plain, false leaders had crept into the Church and corrupted many. Paul's letter of rebuke received scant shrift. In an unsuccessful visit designed to improve matters, Timothy and Paul himself were violently snubbed and probably physically manhandled. They had seen it all.

Models for leadership

Paul does not advocate or embody any one model of leadership. He gives instead a number of telling illustrations to show the way a truly Christian leader will operate. Here are some of them:

The wet nurse (1 Cor. 3.2). Paul had seen the wet nurse looking after an orphaned baby, saving it from death by milk from her own body. That is the sort of thing he had to do in the early days at Corinth among the new believers. Any good leader needs to be able to provide basic nourishment for new Christians without giving them indigestion.

The father (1 Cor. 4.15). Paul seems to have two ideas in mind with this image. First, he insists that Christian leaders must be able to bring men and women to new birth in Christ. Second, they must be able to offer a father's guidance and discipline for young Christians. This remains a crucial aspect of leadership in a permissive and non-directive age.

The example (1 Cor. 4.6f.). Leaders must give a good example. If their lives are not an inducement to discipleship their words will fall on deaf ears.

The clown (1 Cor. 4.10). In a bitingly ironic passage Paul shows he is willing to be mocked, stoned and imprisoned for his Master. He is prepared to be laughed to scorn for his allegiance to an obvious failure, a crucified Messiah. But, as in Shakespeare, it is the clown who in reality is wise, the blind person who alone can see. Amazingly, Paul is willing to adopt and advocate that role for Christian leaders.

The worker (1 Cor. 3.8f.). Christian leadership involves long hours of hard work. It calls for the constant capacity to face disappointment. It calls for persistence, a willingness to cooperate with other workers and partnership with God.

The farmer (1 Cor. 3.6). Whether it be sowing seed, watering it or harvesting it, Christian leaders are called to be involved in the market garden business, not in the preservation of ancient buildings.

The master builder (1 Cor. 3.10). Paul sees himself as a senior Christian worker, helping to raise a spiritual temple. First he seeks to lay the foundation of Christ in every life that will accept it. Then he sets out to build on that foundation a superstructure that will withstand the fire of assessment on judgment day. He knows that if he builds carelessly he could see the temple destroyed by schism or heinous sin among members. His task was to see a corporate temple for God erected in carnal Corinth. And that is the calling of every true Church builder.

The servant (1 Cor. 3.5). As if that was not a revolutionary enough description for a Christian leader, Paul goes further and sees himself as a slave (2 Cor. 4.5). As a slave you might have a kind master or a brute. But in either case you had no money, no rights, no assured prospect of liberation. You were a chattel, not a person. It is astonishing that the New Testament takes this term of universal opprobrium and uses it to describe their total devotion to their Lord.

The steward (1 Cor. 4.1f.). This was a trusted slave given responsibility to order the whole of an ancient household. He would receive daily instructions from his master and see that they were carried out. All his master's resources would be available to him, but he would be accountable for the way he used them. Such is the task of the Christian leader.

The man in the dock (1 Cor. 4.3). Paul is not concerned with what others think of him, or even with his own self-assessment. All that matters is how the Lord will assess him at the end of his life. It is with that goal in mind that he pours himself out for the Corinthians.

The scraping from the saucepan (1 Cor. 4.13). Paul deliberately chooses this astounding simile to describe the degradation he is prepared to endure for the Corinthians. He was in fact facing daily mockery and rejection. We need leaders like that.

The ambassador (2 Cor. 5.20). The leader is an ambassador for Christ, representing his country in an alien land. He has to be fully versed both in his own country's policies and in the culture of the land where he is an ambassador, so as to be able to interpret the one to the other. Moreover, his country is largely judged on the basis of his personal speech and behaviour. It is a most challenging model for any Christian leader.

Those dozen images, almost all from the first few chapters of 1 Corinthians, show the variety and complexity of Paul's understanding of Christian leadership; and they are far from exhaustive. But they suggest that if we entertain any monochrome conception of what Christian leadership means, we are sure to be wrong. It is a many-splendoured thing and it is all derived from Jesus, the leader of men who was servant of all.

Dangers in leadership

These two letters to Corinth provide eloquent illustration of the dangers that beset leaders, and often cripple them. Here are some of them:

The danger of going it alone (1 Cor. 3. 5–6). Clearly some of the Corinthians had been seeing Paul, Apollos and Peter and others as independent operators, each doing his own thing. Paul insists that true pastors cooperate to do God's thing. The plurality and complementarity of leaders is strongly stressed by the apostle, and it needs to be drummed into the modern Church where ministers are normally in sole charge and can be highly individualistic, and indeed authoritarian.

The danger of causing division (1 Cor. 1.12f.). There is no suggestion that Paul, Apollos and others were setting out to create parties for themselves. It was the camp followers who were behaving like football fans and using the names of Christian leaders to express their own need for significance. Leaders need to watch out against becoming a sort of cult figure. It is bad for the leader, disastrous for the Church, and dishonouring to Christ.

The danger of pride (2 Cor. 11.16–21; 12.11; cf. 1 Cor. 3.5). Clearly some Corinthian leaders were boasting of their spiritual pedigree and achievements. Paul cuts at the root of this attitude. All the qualities we have are given us by God, and we should not boast of them any more than we would about our Christmas presents. They are gifts, and we should be thankful for them. That is the attitude Paul seeks to inculcate (1 Cor. 4.7). To enforce it, he does not even speak of Apollos and himself as people, but as God's instruments: 'What, after all, is Apollos?' Pride kills spiritual effectiveness. It is the primal sin. And it is an occupational hazard for gifted leaders.

The danger of discouragement (2 Cor. 4.1, 15). There was much at Corinth to cause Paul distress, even despair. But he tells us that on the whole he did not lose heart. He had obtained mercy from God and that drove him on. He had also received from God the ministry of serving them, and that sustained him through hardships and disappointments.

The danger of deception (2 Cor. 11.3). Paul was faced by apparent colleagues who were nothing of the sort. He had the perception to see through their bombastic talk and recognize them for what they were: 'deceitful workers' (v. 13) masquerading as emissaries of Christ. They appear to have been Jews who were influenced by the florid style of Hellenistic rhetoric. Christian charity among leaders does not dispense with the need for clear thinking and shrewd assessment of potential colleagues.

The danger of overvaluing particular gifts (1 Cor. 12—14). These chapters reveal that spiritual gifts such as tongues and prophecy were high on the spiritual agenda of the Corinthians. But Paul insists that spirituality should not be judged by gifts but by character. The church at Corinth seems to have sought gifts rather than the Giver – a highly dangerous, and very contemporary, failing.

The danger of pursuing acceptable language (1 Cor. 2.4; 1.20f; 4.19f.). Leadership involves talk. And talk can easily become an end in itself, not a stimulus to action. It is easier to preach than to practise! Paul reminds his readers that the kingdom of God does not consist in talk but in power: the power of God to build a church from the riff-raff of Corinth.

The danger of wanting to be popular (1 Cor. 4.1ff.). Paul makes it plain that he is not concerned with what the Corinthians think of him now. What matters is how the Lord thinks of him on judgment day. The Lord, not the Corinthians, will be the judge. Then, and not now, will be the occasion. The hunger for popularity, with its attendant compromises, is a snare which causes the downfall of many a leader.

The danger of wanting crowns without thorns (1 Cor. 4.8). He chides the Corinthians: 'Already you have all you want! Already you have become rich! You have become kings

– and that without us!' This attitude was very dangerous. The wise Christian leader will warn against any theology of resurrection power which does not embrace in equal measure the way of the cross. Those who talk of possessing 'fullness now' tend to become arrogant towards other Christians and increasingly unteachable. They are very unlike their Master, who endured the cross. The cross is the corrective for today's hedonistic society, eager for thrills, for ease, consumed by self-esteem and very reluctant to suffer. The cross exposes wrong ideals of leadership and also shows how they can be transcended.

Requirements in leadership

There are many attributes of good leadership scattered through these two long letters, some of them explicit, some of them culled, quietly, from the apostle's own experience.

The first strikes us at the very outset of the first letter. Paul writes the whole epistle in *the context of grateful prayer* – his thanks to God for the Corinthians, his deep faith, his overflowing confidence. The leader must above all be a man or woman of confident prayer and praise.

A second gift to covet and develop among leaders is *effective communication*. Paul does not always succeed at this; parts of his second letter are particularly obscure. But he is clear that effective speaking and preaching does not rely on eloquence or careful preparation, important though those can be. It is testimony to God that carries weight, and that testimony centres on 'Jesus Christ and him crucified' (1 Cor. 2.2f.). When that happens the Church grows, because people put their faith not in the leaders but in the power of God.

The discovery and fulfilment of your *role* is a very important feature of good leadership. There needs to be a group of leaders in a church or organization – we have already noted the perils of autocracy. But each leader needs to know what areas constitute his strength and particular calling, and what areas do not. Nobody can do everything. The attempt to be the omni-competent leader is bound to fail. I do not think that Paul is denigrating the significance of baptism (1 Cor. 1.17) when he says that God has not called him to baptize but to preach the gospel. He is merely asserting that baptizing people was not his primary sphere of ministry.

Paul himself was an enthusiast. And enthusiasts tend to exaggerate! It is all the more impressive, therefore, to find him extolling the value of *accuracy* (1 Cor. 1.16). A leader has only to be found out exaggerating a few times to lose all credibility.

It would be natural to expect Paul, so well-connected and so educated, to pay particular attention to the prominent people at Corinth. But that is not the case. He stresses *the importance of insignificant members* of the Church: 'Not many of you were wise by human standards; not many were influential; not many were of noble birth' (1 Cor. 1.26). How like God to choose the foolish things in the world to shame the wise, and to bring to nothing the things that are highly esteemed. Just like God, to be sure – but not what we would expect from a top rabbi from the University of Tarsus! Little people matter to God and they should matter to the good leader. It is when people know they matter that they can grow and find their full potential.

A vibrant church is always going to have new Christians joining it. Therefore the leader must be *able to teach*. Paul uses the image of the bottle and the meat (1 Cor. 3.2). People need spiritual food appropriate for their stage of development and the good leader has the responsibility of bringing new believers (irrespective of their natural age) from first sucks on the bottle to the ability to digest strong meat, so that they can begin to discern the mind of Christ and start to act like him. That is the stage of development to which Christian leaders should aim to lead their congregation.

The good leader will be *modest*. He will not blow his own trumpet. His standing will arise from his converts, not from letters of commendation from others (2 Cor. 3.1–3). Alas, some of the most self-confident ministers I have ever met have no converts to refer to!

Leaders need *warmth* if people are truly to embrace them. Cold leadership never wins affection. But when a leader gives himself to his people (2 Cor. 6.12), puts no obstacle in their way (2 Cor. 6.3) and lovingly entreats them not to miss the day of God's grace (2 Cor. 6.1) his followers will reciprocate. There is a fascinating passage in the nineteenth-century Scottish minister James Stalker's book, *The Preacher and His Models,* which underlines the importance of a leader's love for members of the congregation:

> I discovered a thing of which nobody had told me, and which I had not anticipated, but which proved a tremendous aid in doing the work of the ministry. I fell in love with my congregation . . . It made it easy to do anything for my people.

Finally the Christian leader must have *a long perspective.* He has only one life. He will have to leave 'this tent' of human flesh one day (2 Cor. 5.1–5) and will want to make the most of his time in it, while looking with humble confidence to the day when he will be 'at home with the Lord'. There is, of course, nothing smug about this confidence. The pastor knows that he must appear before the judgment seat of Christ and give an account of his stewardship. So his supreme long-term aim is to please the Lord (2 Cor. 5.9–10).

What a standard for leaders is set before us in these Corinthian letters! What shameful imposters those arrogant, self-centred 'super-apostles' are seen to be in the light of it. Authentic Christian leadership is extremely demanding, but it is the greatest privilege to which anyone could aspire.

5

Luke on leadership

————◆————

Luke wrote two major books in the New Testament, the first of which gives us insight into the servant leadership of Jesus, which we have already considered. The second shows the development of the infant Church from tiny beginnings in Jerusalem into a movement poised to capture the ancient world. How does he envisage the leadership which energized the movement? Much that has been written on this subject, seeking to validate one or another model of leadership in the subsequent Church, rests on rather insecure foundations.

Apostles. It was Jesus who instituted the apostolic office, and they are in some sense an echo of the 12 tribes of Israel, commissioned to lead the new people of God into effectiveness. Clearly apostles act like the Old Testament *shelichim*, authorized delegates, whom Jesus put in place to continue his work after he had left them. They are the supreme authorities in the Church: the Church's doctrine and fellowship is called the apostles' doctrine and fellowship. Yet they appear very seldom in the Acts. They are shadowy figures: only Peter and John emerge from obscurity. We do not know what became of Matthias whom they appointed to join them after the suicide of Judas. We do not know for certain if they called anyone else 'apostle' in addition to the Eleven: Barnabas and Saul are only called 'apostles' in Acts 14 during the first missionary journey when they are 'sent out' (the root of the Greek word 'apostle') from the Antioch church. The authority of the apostles clearly derived from their close association with Jesus (Acts 1.22f.). Their role to act as guarantors of the continuity between the Jesus of history and the Christ of faith was by definition unrepeatable. They never contemplated a succession – in Judaism when the *shaliach's* commission was completed, it returned to the sender; he could not pass it on. So we never find them creating apostles after them, though in the Pauline epistles we occasionally read of 'apostles of the churches', meaning representatives of one church visiting another, and it is sometimes used in this sense today. But the apostles of Jesus Christ were unique. Their primary tasks were to evangelize and plant churches, to safeguard the teaching of the Church, and to give themselves to ministering God's word and prayer. We would love to know more. But Acts does not satisfy our curiosity.

Presbyters. Presbyters (the word from which our English 'priest' is derived: it had nothing to do with the Old Testament sacrificing priest) appear without introduction in 11.30 as 'the elders' in Jerusalem. In Judaism elders were laymen who saw the law observed in the synagogues: they probably provided a convenient model for the Christians to take over. We find them all over the Mediterranean basin. In Acts they appear in Jerusalem and Ephesus, and Saul and Barnabas appointed them in every church on their first missionary journey (14.23). We may take it, then, that elders were the regular local leaders of the churches. Their function was to be *episkopoi* (20.28), a word from which we derive 'bishop' and which means 'overseers'. In Acts 20 it is explicitly stated that these 'overseers' of verse 28 are the 'elders' of verse 17. The two are identical. Elder is their title and oversight their function. We are not told if they were ordained by the laying on of hands. Probably they were, as this was the normal Jewish custom. We learn more about them from other parts of the New Testament, but not from Luke.

Deacons. If we look for 'deacons' in Acts, we shall look in vain. In Acts 6 poor relief takes the form of 'deaconing tables' while preaching is 'deaconing the word'. The Seven mentioned here are never called deacons: they were a board of almoners set up to meet a particular need.

It is hard to avoid the conclusion that there is a very undeveloped view of ministry in Acts. We do not find the 'threefold ministry' of bishops, priests and deacons. We discover little about the apostles themselves. But we do find a fair amount about people like Agabus; or the prophesying daughters of Philip; about James, who sprang to prominence although not a member of the apostolic band; about Stephen, who was such a charismatic leader, innovative thinker and courageous martyr; and about Saul of Tarsus, whom nobody but God ever ordained.

If, then, we persist in asking traditional questions of Luke about leadership in Acts, we shall continue to receive unsatisfactory answers. There is simply not enough material to go on. But what if we start asking a very different question, and enquire what Luke believed was important about Christian leadership? Then we get a very clear answer.

Principles of Christian leadership

What, then, has Luke to say about leadership?

Leadership is a gift of God. Luke is crystal clear about this. Leadership is not some office for which we can apply. A leader is someone whom God raises up. That is how the Twelve came into leadership: Jesus himself called them. Their leadership came from divine election. So did Paul's. That is exceedingly obvious. But it is also true of Philip, Barnabas, Silas and the others whom we meet in the pages of Acts. Their leadership did not spring from any role they played, or human authorization they received: it was a God-given facility. The same is true of the Ephesian elders. It was 'the Holy Spirit who has made you overseers'. While therefore there is no opposition between *charisma* and office in the Lucan writings, as there was later on in the Church, it is plain that for Luke the divine *charisma* was the prerequisite for anyone exercising leadership in the Church. You did not receive the Holy Spirit for the task of 'deaconing tables', for example, *after* the apostles had laid hands on you: you simply were not considered for the job unless you had *already* shown signs of being filled with the Holy Spirit (Acts 6. 5–6). That is the opposite way round from our contemporary practice, where the act of ordination is often assumed to provide the spiritual enabling. Alas, it will not do so, as many powerless ministries demonstrate, unless the divine call and enabling is already there.

Leadership is shared. The second important thing about leadership in Acts is that it is shared. The leaders do not operate solo: they work in teams. 'The elders' are always plural in Acts, as in the rest of the New Testament. Peter and John worked together. So did Paul and Barnabas, Barnabas and Mark, Paul and Silas, Paul and Timothy. There is no single presbyter in charge at Antioch (13.1). They are a team of five. Shared leadership has obvious strengths. A team demonstrates the fellowship of leadership. It is an example of the small group of loving and praying friends that can so helpfully be reproduced at various levels in a congregation. It preserves the church from imbalance and the undue dependence on a single leader. It preserves the individual leader from megalomania and from burnout. It was a very wise arrangement. But in many modern churches it simply does not happen. There is one person in overall charge. The congregation's attitude is 'We have hired you. We expect you to get on with it, with a little help from us.' And from that fundamental flaw flows loneliness in ministry, exhaustion, blinkered vision, and polarization between pastor and people.

He is glad to have a little stage to play on. They are glad to let him, because they can then criticize him in peace, and can be spared the inconvenience of undue commitment.

Leadership is diverse. The third characteristic of leadership, as portrayed by Luke in Acts, is that it falls into clear categories. There is the circulating, superintending, church-planting ministry represented by the apostles and their associates: Barnabas, Silas, Paul, Philip, and to some extent Agabus and Apollos. And then there is the settled, local leadership that emerges or is appointed in the local churches – the 'elders' at Jerusalem, Ephesus or Antioch. This pattern continued into the second century when travelling teachers and prophets serviced the local leadership of presbyters. The idea of the leaders in the local church being respected local Christians is so obvious that it is amazing that so few main-line churches have adopted it. They have left it to the fast-growing independent churches which generally recruit their leadership from within their own number. But it makes so much sense to appoint experienced local Christians who have shown their mettle over a number of years. They need to equipped, of course, and that is where the mobile circulating ministry comes in. They can provide short courses, offer wise counsel to the local leaders, and preserve the catholicity of the Church. But the local Christians, who have shown their talents and commitment during their time in the congregation, would be respected and loved as they move into leadership.

Leadership is service. A fourth aspect of leadership which Luke stresses is its servant nature. The leaders are not above the Church, to dominate it. They are, if you like, beneath it to serve it. That is how Jesus served his little band of followers. And he told them, in words which are important for Luke (22.25f.):

> The kings of the Gentiles lord it over them; and those who exer
> cise authority over them call themselves Benefactors. But you

are not to be like that. Instead the greatest among you should be like the youngest, and the one who rules like the one who serves.

That is the model of leadership being exercised by the apostles in Jerusalem, by the Seven to the widows, by Philip to the eunuch, by Paul and Silas to the jailer. It was a servant ministry through and through. They gained respect not by demanding it, but by earning it. Theirs was the unanswerable authority of a leadership which gives and serves and loves. They saw leadership not as a status which deserved honour but as an opportunity to provide service and meet need: in short, they operated as the representatives of Jesus the Servant.

Leadership is broadly based. A fifth fascinating characteristic seems to have been that those whom we would call 'Charismatic' and 'non-Charismatic' functioned in the same shared leadership teams. Antioch is the most obvious example. The leadership at Antioch consisted of five men drawn from widely different national and cultural backgrounds (Acts 13.1ff.). Some of them were prophets, some teachers. On the whole those two categories do not find it easy to work together. The teacher finds the prophet unpredictable, emotional, perhaps wild and a little dangerous. The prophet finds the teacher over-prepared, bookish, predictable and a little dull. And yet prophets and teachers were working as a team in Antioch, as they were in Caesarea and Jerusalem. Does that not have something important to say to our modern Church, which is often polarized over the Charismatic issue, and tends as a result either to go short on good teaching or else lack inspiration and immediacy? We need both. Happy the church that is big enough in its sympathies to accommodate both.

Leadership is learned on the job. A sixth feature of the early Christian leadership which Luke paints for us is this. He makes it abundantly clear that they trained people on the job, not in some primitive attempt at a college. It is no good saying that there were no colleges available to them. They improvised many things, and could have improvised this had they thought it was needful. The Christians could have taken over the rabbinic schools, just as they took over and adapted the system of synagogue presbyters. But these apostles knew that you do not train people behind desks and in libraries. You train them in the heat of battle and with real encounters. This is one of the strengths of the Oxford Centre for Christian Apologetics. Carefully chosen candidates spend a year at this college, but a good deal of their training is in their placements and in the evangelistic missions held in British universities. It is there that they meet the real issues: atheism, sexual perversion, concern about suffering and other faiths, scepticism about the gospels and the resurrection. They sink or swim by the way they handle these real issues. That is how I seek to train younger evangelists – taking them with me to missions in England and Europe.

You rarely get good ministers in a church if the only way you train them is to remove them from their homes, send them to a college where they prepare with *book* learning for an *oral* ministry. Of course, there is a genuine need for colleges to exist and to train to a high standard the next generation of scholars and academics. But there is no less need for the colleges to run short sandwich courses to equip those who have already shown some signs of leadership in particular areas. We have already noted the speed at which St Mellitus, the college associated with Holy Trinity Brompton, is attracting large numbers of students for its mixed-mode courses, with part of the week in college and part in the workplace. This is a great step in the right direction which some other colleges are trying to follow.

There is, of course, another way of approaching the issue. Dr Lindsay Brown, erstwhile head of the worldwide International

Fellowship of Evangelical Students, tells me of a conversation he once had with the legendary Dr Martyn Lloyd-Jones. Lindsay was newly graduated from Oxford at the time, and asked his advice. Would he benefit from formal theological training? To his surprise, Lloyd-Jones said 'No. There is a huge difference between being trained theologically in technical terms, and learning to think theologically. With the benefit of a good university education, you should have been taught how to think critically and analytically.' He advised Lindsay to keep up his reading, and meet with an older Christian minister once a month. Lindsay did all that for some 25 years and he is the living proof of the value of that type of training. But to suppose that a young man or woman straight from university and a closed college system will be any good in a position of leadership after spending three years in a seminary is certainly testing fortune. Sometimes, in the providence of God, it works. Often, predictably, it does not.

These six principles come out very clearly in the book of Acts. They are fundamental to the quality of leadership that we meet in this exciting book, and which, sadly, is often missing in the leadership of some modern churches.

6

Qualities of a leader

We have not yet done with Luke's material. He can help us, I believe, discover what sort of questions went through the minds of early Christian leaders as they sought possible replacements and additions to their ranks. I believe that is the main reason why Luke gives us the moving and detailed account of Paul's farewell to the Ephesian elders in Acts 20. He is showing us what Christian leadership meant for Paul, what he wanted to see in those elders at Ephesus, and what he hoped would characterize Christian leaders down the years until Jesus comes again.

Here, then, are some of the questions about the qualities to be sought in Christian leaders, to which Acts 20 provides a clue. They are questions we would do well to ask today about any applicants for Christian leadership.

Are they humble?

Are they small enough for God to use? Not big enough, you notice, but small enough. Paul has worked three years among these believers in Ephesus, the longest time he spent anywhere. He is now about to leave them for (he thinks) the last time and wants to assure himself of the qualities instilled in them. So he reminds them that ever since he came into the province of Asia he has served the Lord with all humility – and they know it (v. 19). It is great to be able credibly to make a claim like that, especially if you were everywhere celebrated as the apostle to the Gentiles. Actually, it is critical. Unless there is this fundamental dedication to the Lord all Christian leadership is sham.

But it is all too possible to be in leadership in the modern Church without that passionate commitment to the Lord. There can be the desire to serve him without the prior humility of allowing him to serve us. There can be a worthy but inadequate humanitarian concern for needy people. There can even be some spiritual pride. People go into Christian leadership for all manner of reasons. But there is only one reason that will bear the weight put upon it. And that is a call from Jesus Christ, a deep love for him, and a passionate determination humbly to serve him and those committed to us.

Do they believe in shared ministry?

There is no room today for the 'one-man band'. Nor was there in the first century. As we have seen, presbyters were always plural. And so they are in Ephesus (v. 17). But in our situation today we place unwarranted pressures on people by expecting them to exercise a one-person ministry. This is both unbiblical and misguided, as I have suggested above. I would want to ask any applicants for Christian leadership today whether or not they believe in shared ministry. This includes the shared ministry of men and women.

To be sure we do not find clear evidence of women presbyters in the New Testament. But we do find that Jesus' attitude to women was utterly revolutionary. We do find women being the first witnesses of the resurrection, and the first to announce it to the men. We do find women deacons. We do find the conviction that in Christ there is neither male nor female (Gal. 3.28). We do find women owning and using Christian homes in the cause of the gospel (12.12). We do find women like Euodia and Syntyche working as fellow labourers with Paul in the gospel (Phil. 4.2). We will return to this subject in the next chapter. For now the question is insistent. Does the candidate for leadership believe in shared leadership?

It is imperative to recognize that God uses teams, and that women as well as men have some place in Christian leadership. Our first-century forebears were enormously courageous in contending against the male chauvinism of their day. We need to follow their example.

Can they inspire others?

The function of leadership is often described in the New Testament by the word *proistasthai:* 'to go out in front'. It may mean going out on a limb. It certainly means to inspire and challenge. Leaders need to lead. There is no doubt that Paul was such a leader. 'I consider my life worth nothing to me', he says (Acts 20.24), and men follow a leader like that. The leaders we meet in Acts, like Stephen, Peter, Paul, John, Philip, all had the gift of inspiring others.

But many of those who are nurtured in our seminaries have no proven gift of leadership. Nobody knows if they can inspire others. They have never been tested.

It is not a question selection boards ask. But it is very important. There is nothing more frustrating for a congregation than to have a minister who is somewhat unsure of his faith, unskilled in training others, unwilling to engage in evangelism, and incompetent to teach attractively within the congregation. In one of her novels P. D. James observed that the most that can be hoped for from a sermon was to survive it. That is not the principle on which the first Christian community operated!

What about their prayer life?

The prayer life of Paul is phenomenal. It shines through this passage. He had for years prayed *for* his young leaders, night and day – accompanied at times by tears (Acts 20.31). And now as he bids farewell to them, we find him on the beach praying *with* them (20.36). To pray both for people and with people will be natural for us if prayer is a real priority in our lives. I saw an email only yesterday from a QC in New Zealand to my son, telling him of the times I had met him when a student in the High Street in Oxford and had stopped to pray. I have no such recollection myself, because it is normal for me to pray with people as we meet. Prayer tends to be much more central in countries like Uganda, South Korea and Latin America than in the West where we have so many other resources that prayer tends to get squeezed out. Not so Paul. The first paragraph of almost all his letters shows what a top priority prayer and thanksgiving was for the apostle. Without prayer we are powerless. Without prayer we cannot lead others. One of the first questions I would want to ask anyone who was being considered for leadership is this: tell me about your prayer life. If they are not steeped in prayer, they will inevitably wilt as the heat and pressures of the ministry take their toll. If there is any lesson that needs to be imprinted on church leadership today, it is the vital importance of prayer.

Is their lifestyle exemplary?

It is hard to exaggerate the importance of example in leadership. You cannot ask people to do things you are not prepared to do and be yourself. Paul is not embarrassed about the example he has shown these young followers of his. His life has been open to inspection at every point, over a number of years (20.19, 31).

It has been consistent (v. 18), dedicated (v. 24), humble (v. 19), persistent in the face of pressures internal and external (v. 19), hardworking (v. 34) and bold (v. 22). He had not *told* them to support the weak. He had *shown* them (v. 35). The quality of his example was such that these people would do anything for him. He was a man of warmth and prayer (v. 36), of generosity and practical labour (v. 34), a man full of the Spirit and devoted to the gospel of God's grace (v. 23f.). One could go on. The whole passage is eloquent about the example of this great Christian leader who was about to pass on the torch to the next generation. They were anxious to pick it up primarily because of what they had seen in him. It is sad when Christian leaders are cited in the press for child abuse, fraud, adultery or lies. What we are speaks more loudly than what we say. There is nothing a church needs more than the godly example of its leaders, leaders who are godly when nobody is looking as well as when they are on show!

What do they believe?

This is a critical question to bear in mind when considering suitability for Christian leadership. Does the candidate genuinely believe the faith of the New Testament? Paul is very explicit about what he believes. He is supremely concerned to testify to the free, unmerited favour of God, 'grace' as he calls it (v. 24), and to urge upon his hearers the appropriate response of repentance and faith (v. 21). It is never easy to preach repentance because human nature is so proud, so turned in on itself, but Paul has not been selective in his teaching at Ephesus. He has taught them the whole counsel of God as he understood it from the Old Testament Scriptures and from the life and teaching of Jesus. It is all too easy to fail in this area. If we proclaim the whole truth apart from whatever flies in the face of contemporary errors and prejudices, we are not preaching the gospel of Christ. Many modern preachers are so afraid of ruffling feathers that they never address contentious issues in their preaching. Real leadership is not afraid to do that if necessary.

When Paul bade farewell to the Ephesian elders he committed them to God: that is natural enough (v. 32). We might do the same. But if you were to add one more thing to 'God' in your commendation, what would it be? For Paul it was the 'word' of God, that is to say, his revelation in Scripture. Why? Because Scripture does not contain man's ideas about God but God's ideas about man and his salvation. This is what the proposed leader is called to preach. And it has great value. It can build up believers, as milk and then meat build up the body. And it can also 'give' people their inheritance among God's people – in the sense of opening their eyes to the spiritual wealth God has in store for them. It is crucial therefore that this 'word' is prominent in personal devotion, group study and public preaching. We need leaders committed to God and his Word.

Can they teach?

Paul certainly could. His teaching was outstanding. He majored on the young leaders (v. 28) and he fed them the Word (v. 32). He did not shrink from unpalatable truth (v. 27) and he clearly denounced false teaching (v. 29). But there was nothing strident about him. He loved those Ephesians dearly, and they knew it (v. 36f.).

In the list of qualities requisite in Christian leaders in Titus chapter 1 and 1 Timothy chapter 3, there is, as we shall see, one requirement, and one only, that is not a moral quality. The candidate must be *didaktikos*, 'able to teach'. If not, he or she will suffer much frustration in the ministry of the Church – and so will the congregation.

As we have seen, Paul taught first by example, but then by public proclamation. I have been very struck in recent years by the paucity of public proclamation of the Christian faith. Thankfully, it happens in almost all the British universities through the Christian Unions, their work throughout the year, but especially in their Events Weeks which engage attractively and fearlessly with current scepticism. This student work is now growing fast on the continent of Europe. But, universities apart, there is not a lot of public proclamation in the UK at large. Sadly, Christians are evacuating the public square.

Paul was also skilled at teaching 'from house to house'. This involves visiting. Unless the pastor knows from personal observation the home life of his congregation, his preaching will be ill applied and will lack relevance. Visiting has fallen into disuse, and we are the poorer for it in church life. What is more, the vast majority of people who do not go to church are also the poorer. They do not know that anyone cares, because nobody bothers to visit them in the name of Christ.

There is another way of translating the Greek *kat'oikous* (v. 20). It may mean 'in houses'. If so it suggests home meetings for exploring and teaching the faith. This was certainly much used in apostolic days, and has been throughout the history of the Church. Richard Baxter, the famous Puritan pastor, reckoned that he did far more good by the home meetings he instituted than in all his public preaching. Facilitating such groups is an important skill for the leader to acquire. Preparing material for them, and being willing to stand aside and let them operate on their own, requires different skills from public teaching of the faith. But these skills are important in an age which is allergic to dogmatic utterances from whatever quarter.

People much prefer to work things out for themselves. Leaders must be 'apt to teach' in a variety of ways.

What is their attitude to money?

As a free-born Roman citizen Paul left a considerable fortune when he became a Christian leader. As such he had no regular income apart from what he earned in tent-making and from occasional gifts. He might well have been tempted to avarice.

But if he was, he overcame the temptation conclusively. 'I have not coveted anyone's silver or gold or clothing' (v. 33). His own hard work provided enough not only for his own necessities (not luxuries) but for those who accompanied him and presumably did not have skills that could be used in almost any location, like tent-making (v. 34).

The love of money remains a great lure for Christian leaders. It accounts for the downfall of some. There is a dangerous tendency in some quarters to require payment for preaching a sermon. Ministers are anxious to be as well paid as other middle-class professionals. Paul was so reliable and so unselfish over money that he could amass a very considerable collection from the Gentile churches to bring up to Jerusalem, without being suspected of malpractice. Integrity with money is a must for any leader.

Can they endure hard times and suffering?

The story of Paul's ministry is the story of suffering. He had been opposed, vilified, beaten, shipwrecked, attacked, and at times left for dead as he blazed the trail of Christ across the Middle East:

> And now, compelled by the Spirit, I am going to Jerusalem, not knowing what will happen to me there. I only know that

in every city the Holy Spirit warns me that prison and hardships are facing me. However, I consider my life worth nothing to me, if only I may finish the race and complete the task the Lord Jesus has given me – the task of testifying to the gospel of God's grace.

(Acts 20.22–24)

Here was a man no hardships could deter from what he believed the Lord was calling him to.

Recently I read of a modern example of a missionary couple facing hardship but also witnessing great fruit. They said that when they arrived in their chosen country, the road from the airport was dark, and the air thick and polluted. The apartment was cold and filthy. They found a heap of soiled sheets in the closet. The bed was a cloth-covered board. They survived the first night dressed in their clothes to stay warm. Next day they saw a small cross on a nearby building. A young woman at the door exclaimed 'We love Jesus very much.' They were invited in, fed and made welcome. The local gutter cleaners were also invited in and soon they were all singing praise to God. As it was a country where persecution was rife, one young woman asked if coming to the house would be dangerous for the inhabitants. 'Oh no', said the host, 'we are too many.' As one man observed, 'It is unstoppable.' That is the sort of leader whom people will follow through hell and high water.

Are they wholehearted?

If someone undertakes Christian leadership for the financial rewards, the prestige, the popularity, or simply as a suitable job, the result will be disastrous. Nothing less than wholehearted commitment will suffice. For leadership is hard. Disappointments abound. There will be many reverses. The temptation to give it all up will sometimes be strong. It is going to require someone who is prepared to work hard: 'these hands of mine have supplied my own needs and the needs of my companions' (20.34). It is going to require some sleepless nights: 'Remember that for three years I never stopped warning each of you night and day with tears' (v. 31). It is going to call for deep care for 'the church of God, which he bought with his own blood' (v. 28). It is going to require wholeheartedness.

We need to relax and have fun, of course, or we shall become dull and overwrought. But there needs to burn within us a deep commitment to accomplishing the task committed to us. The Christian community needs a leadership that is there not for the money or for a job, but for the Lord; a leadership that counts it the most privileged employment on earth.

Are they able to accept ministry from others?

If leaders are going to be a real help to hurting people they cannot appear to be immune to the pressures and pains that engulf them. But leaders do sometimes give that impression of invulnerability. If you do not believe me, go and listen to a group of ministers meeting together and talking about their work. You will very rarely hear them admitting failure. They seem to feel that if they open up and come off their pedestal their lives will be shattered. But that is precisely what is needed. People in the congregation will relate far more honestly and gladly to a leader who is 'touched with the feeling of their infirmities'. Leaders need not fear that to admit their own pressures and failings will diminish the respect in which they are held: on the contrary, it will generally enhance it. And it will mean that others will be able to get close enough to the leader to love and encourage him. It will further encourage honesty and integrity in the congregation. Leaders need never be ashamed of being seen as wounded healers. After all, that is what their Master was. Paul, too, was willing to accept ministry from his peers and indeed his juniors in the Christian life. 'They all wept as they embraced him and kissed him. What grieved them most was his statement that they would never see his face again. Then they accompanied him to the ship' (20.36). Happy the leader who, like Paul, can gratefully accept the ministry that those in his congregation delight to bring.

Are they truly open to the Holy Spirit?

That is the vital ingredient in all radical leadership. The true leader needs to be so full of the Holy Spirit that it is not so much his leadership as that of the Spirit in and through him. This is strongly emphasized in the book of Acts, but it is not so much emphasized today, so it is well to close this chapter with it. Paul allows himself to be 'compelled by the Spirit' (20.22). He is sensitively listening for the quiet voice of the Spirit, even if that voice tells him things he would not have thought of or would rather not hear – in Paul's case that imprisonment and afflictions await him (v. 23). He is not only full of the Spirit, sensitive to the Spirit, but determined to obey the Spirit. And that is something Paul longs to see in his young assistants, as they take over the leadership of the church in Ephesus. It is the Holy Spirit who has made them overseers. If they are to lead, they must do so in the wisdom, the love, the courage and the power which he supplies. There is no substitute for Christian leaders who are full of the Holy Spirit.

These are some of the leadership qualities set before us by Luke in this wonderful chapter. They may serve to remind us that, contrary to the claims of some commentators, the requirements for leadership in the primitive Church were not crude or rudimentary; they were very demanding. If we asked these kinds of questions when considering men and women for the ordained ministry of the Christian churches we might find ourselves with fewer disasters and a great deal more effectiveness in ministerial ranks.

7

Women in leadership

It was not that I was a male chauvinist pig. It was simply that I had not considered the matter much.

When I became principal of St John's Theological College, Nottingham, I quite naturally appointed women as well as men on to the staff, and needless to say they taught mostly men.

When I was rector of St Aldate's, Oxford, I had women as well as men on the staff team and they were all free to operate according to their gifting in every respect, except celebrating Communion, which no lay persons did. The women members of the team felt affirmed and appreciated. So it was no big deal.

But it rapidly became one.

Attitudes among evangelicals hardened. Scriptures were thrown about to suggest that women must not teach or lead in mixed company, that male headship was everywhere required for teaching the faith, and that the apostle Paul clearly forbade women to teach ('I do not permit a woman to teach or to have authority over a man', 1 Tim. 2.12). And because the same arguments are still used today in some quarters by those who want to be guided by Scripture, it seems worth explaining how I came to disagree rather strongly with what appeared to me to be the inconsistencies, assumptions and exegesis brought to bear.

Inconsistencies

Let's take the inconsistencies first. If it were really a matter of Christian conviction that a woman was inherently not intended by God to teach or to exercise authority over men, then the Christians who held that view ought to be protesting strongly when we have a woman queen, a woman prime minister, chief constable, or a woman heading a business or writing a book.

I heard no such complaints. They should have complained vigorously when, say, Christina Baxter was made principal of St John's Theological College. However, I heard no such complaints. And I find it most repugnant of all when conservative Christians do not allow a woman to teach in their pulpit while they are perfectly happy for a woman missionary to teach mixed audiences, to baptize and indeed to lead the Communion, so long as it is far away on the 'mission field'. This 'out of sight, out of mind' attitude is reprehensible.

Assumptions

How about some of the assumptions that lie behind the male leadership cause?

One is taken over uncritically from secular life: it is that authority is all about calling the shots. By contrast, in the attitude of Jesus, authority is all about service:

> You know that those who are regarded as rulers of the Gentiles lord it over them, and their high officials exercise authority over them. Not so with you. Instead, whoever wants to become great among you must be your servant, and whoever wants to be first must be slave of all. For even the Son of Man did not come to be served but to serve, and to give his life as a ransom for many.

> (Mark 10.42–45)

Secular feminism centres on gaining equal rights. Biblical feminism centres on having equal opportunity to serve.

Another assumption is that all women need to be in submission to men, and this is often taken to include single women. There are indeed several injunctions in the New Testament for wives to submit to their husbands, and we will look at that later, but there is not a single command for women in general to submit to men. The only possible exception is 1 Corinthians 11.3, 'the head of the woman is [the] man', where the Greek is ambiguous and I will turn to it later.

A third assumption is often made that you cannot find women exercising ministerial leadership in the Bible. But you can! Miriam, Deborah and Huldah were striking examples in the Old Testament. This was certainly not because there were no competent males available. And in contrast to the male attitude prevalent in Judaism where a man thanked God daily that 'he has not made me a Gentile, a slave or a woman' we find Jesus (and the New Testament generally) adopting a revolutionary attitude to women. He respected them, welcomed them, and had them among his close associates. They were there at the cross when the men had run away, and Jesus made them the first witnesses of the resurrection, charged with the responsibility of informing the male disciples that Jesus was risen. This is all the more remarkable when we recall that Jewish society at that time would not allow the testimony of a woman to stand in court. How splendidly like God to entrust the message of the greatest event in world history to women to pass on! It is therefore not surprising that in the New Testament we find a number of women entrusted with ministry and leadership. There was Phoebe, a deacon of the church at Cenchrea on the Corinthian isthmus (Rom. 16.1), clearly an office of substantial responsibility. She is also called *prostatis*, a patron, a woman set over others who were what the Romans called her *clients* and looked to her for assistance of various sorts. She was clearly an influential woman in society who also occupied a leadership role in church. Then there were Priscilla and Aquila, a husband and wife team very active in ministry. Four times out of the six in the New Testament the woman's name is mentioned first. Is that significant? Another married couple were Andronicus and Junia (Rom. 16.7) who are said to be outstanding among the apostles – this phrase was interpreted (possibly wrongly!) by the patristic writers as indicating that they themselves exercised an apostolic role. Tryphena, Tryphosa, Persis and Mary (Rom. 16.6, 12) are all commended for their Christian work, presumably in ministry of some sort. Nympha hosted a house church (Col. 4.15). Euodia and Syntyche were fellow workers with Paul (Phil. 4.2–3): they 'contended at my side in the cause of the gospel'. Philip had four daughters who exercised the gift of prophecy (Acts 21.9), and then there was the mysterious 'elect lady' to whom 2 John was addressed. So the assumption that women did not exercise leadership in New Testament times is clearly mistaken.

A fourth assumption is that women are ruled out of leadership because Jesus chose only male apostles. Though true for his day in his society, this may well have no bearing on the future leadership of God's people. We might as well ask why Jesus did not choose any Gentiles to be apostles! It seems that he chose the Twelve with profound symbolism. They were to be the founders of his new Israel, just as the 12 patriarchs had been of the old. Jesus lived between the old covenant and the new. The new would usher in the complete equality of all people, men and women, slaves and free, Jews and Gentiles in Christ (Gal. 3.28). This is part of the inheritance of our redemption: it does away with all divisions of race, class and gender.

From wrong assumptions we turn to questionable exegesis.

Exegesis

1 'Headship': 1 Corinthians 11.3

'I want you to realise that the head of every man is Christ, and the head of the woman is [the] man, and the head of Christ is God.' Remember that the Greek words for 'woman' and 'man' are the same as for 'wife' and 'husband', and the latter makes much better sense here. But there is considerable uncertainty about what the writer means, and the verse has been taken in two very different and contrasting ways.

It is just possible that the Greek word *kephale* means 'source' as in the source of life, source of a river. In classical writers this is sometimes the case. If so this could be a statement about men and women in general. Thus God the Father is the source of the human Jesus Christ, Christ as agent in creation is the source of humankind, and man is the source of woman ('the rib he had taken out of the man', Gen. 2.21). This interpretation could be supported by 11.8, 'man did not come from woman but woman from man'. If this understanding of *kephale* is correct, there is no suggestion of woman's subordination. Paul says nothing here of the man's authority, but rather that without the crowning glory of the woman man is not complete (11.7).

However, despite much learned discussion, it is more probable that Paul is talking about the relation between husband and wife (as in the very similar passage in Eph. 5.21ff.). Moreover the Greek *kephale,* 'head', has not been conclusively shown to mean 'source' anywhere in the New Testament. As in Ephesians 1.22; 4.15, Colossians 1.18; 2.10, 'head' indicates that the person referred to has been endowed with authority in the particular situation under discussion. And remember the radical new kingdom perspective on authority. To be appointed as head does not mean that you have the authority to domineer, but rather the responsibility to serve. It is just possible that Paul

71

is setting out a hierarchy in this verse (God-Christ-husband-wife) but if so, he obscures his point by beginning with the middle relationship within the hierarchy rather than at one end or the other. Moreover 'headship' is not linked to 'authority' in this passage. The only time 'authority' is mentioned it belongs to the woman (v. 10), and mutuality and interdependence between the sexes is explicit in verses 11 and 12: the only 'subordination' is of both sexes to God. In any case, this whole passage (11.1–16) is not about headship but about public worship in the Corinthian church, especially about women and veils. Headship means there is order and distinctiveness within the relationship. It is quite illegitimate to expound the husband/wife relationship in any way that cannot be paralleled by the God/Christ relationship, where there is clearly equality of life, but differentiation of function. So it is with men and women, and especially husbands and wives. They are equal before God but not identical to each other. Within the marriage bond there is a proper lead which the husband should give, always remembering that this is for the better serving of his wife.

The word 'submit' is one we do not enjoy these days, but the New Testament is clear that the Church should submit to Christ, and Christians should submit to one another. The chauvinists who love to quote Ephesians 5.22, 'Wives, submit to your husbands', should start with the previous verse, 'Submit *to one another* out of reverence for Christ.' Paul goes on to show what the wife's submission looks like – deferring to her husband, cleaving to him, and respecting him. But then he shows what the husband's form of submission is like – he must protect his wife, sacrifice himself for her, and cherish her as his own body – just as Christ did all three for the Church. The *form* submission takes for husband and wife is different, but it is just as challenging for them both. And neither is demeaning.

Surrender to self-giving love is not painful, and only self-giving love merits anything of the sort. What a glaring contrast this submission to love gives us compared with the accepted pattern in today's society of asserting your rights!

2 Women are to be silent: 1 Corinthians 14.33–35

> As in all the congregations of the saints, women should remain silent in the churches. They are not allowed to speak, but must be in submission, as the Law says. If they want to enquire about something, they should ask their own husbands at home, for it is disgraceful for a woman to speak in the church.

At first sight this looks very negative. Nevertheless it cannot possibly be taken at first sight! The law never enjoins silence on women, and Paul has already (11.5) permitted women not only to pray aloud but also to prophesy in church. They are not restricted to a passive role in worship but may take a leading, vocal part. Incidentally, there is some uncertainty about the authenticity of these verses, as Gordon Fee's magisterial commentary on 1 Corinthians (Eerdmans, 1987, p. 699ff.) points out.

But assuming they are original, how can we reconcile these two strongly contrasting passages in the same letter, permitting and forbidding women to speak? It is not very difficult. The world Paul uses for 'speak', *lalein*, has been employed a good deal in this chapter for 'to speak in tongues'. It may be that he is discouraging women from undisciplined and indiscriminate speaking in tongues during the services and so creating disorder. That would be disgraceful. But it is not necessary so to construe it. The Corinthian assemblies were on any showing chaotic. Remember *gune* can mean either woman or wife. Here the context is unambiguous. Paul is forbidding wives to chatter in the assembly, not women as such to speak. It would indeed be a disgrace for the wives to make a lot of disturbance by asking endless questions of their husbands. In those days women received no education so would naturally ask more questions than the men. Let them not chatter away in church (*lalein* is often used for informal chattering) but let them ask their questions of their husbands when they return home. This injunction is perfectly compatible with allowing a woman to pray or prophesy or take some other part in the meeting. It certainly does not mean that a woman must be entirely silent.

3 Women are not allowed to teach: 1 Timothy 2.11–15

'I do not permit a woman to teach or to have authority over a man; she must be silent' (1 Tim. 2.12). Paul bases this on the priority of Adam's creation over Eve's, and the fact that Eve was deceived by the serpent, while Adam was not deceived – simply disobedient. The role the apostle sees for women is childbearing, faith, love and holiness with modesty. Surely that is decisive. But is it?

First, notice that once again we have the ambiguity. Does Paul mean wife and husband by *gune* and *aner*? Or does he mean woman and man? Probably, in this context, the latter.

Second, it cannot be an absolute command against all women teaching anywhere. Paul himself allowed women to teach at least women and children (Titus 2.3–5; 2 Tim.1.5). This itself would be strange if, as is sometimes argued, women are especially prone to deception. Why should Paul let such flawed women loose on women and children, and thus harm them? It is also ironic, for Paul indicates that Timothy's competence in the Scriptures is largely due to his mother and grandmother! Moreover, Paul allows women to prophesy (1 Cor. 11.5). We know Priscilla taught, and of course in Revelation we meet Jezebel (2.20). The church is told to reject her not because she is a woman but because of the evil content of her teaching. Since women are found teaching (Acts 18.26), prophesying (Acts 21.8; 1 Cor. 11.5), and labouring in the gospel (Phil. 4.3) among the Pauline churches, we can be confident that this passage in 1Timothy cannot be a blanket prohibition. It seems to relate to a particular situation in Ephesus, where Timothy is supervising the church. What could that be?

Both letters to Timothy make it plain that certain women were very troublesome at Ephesus (1 Tim. 5.11–15, and particularly 2 Tim. 3.6–9). We read of women who are 'loaded down with sins and are swayed by all kinds of evil desires, always learning but never able to acknowledge the truth'; women who 'get into the habit of being idle and going about from house to house. And not only do they become idlers but also gossips and busybodies, saying things they ought not to'. Against such a background is it any wonder the apostle wants to stop such women from disturbing the church?

Unstable and doctrinally unsound women seem to have formed a substantial part of the headway being made in Ephesus by false teachers. It is hardly surprising that Paul sees such women as deceived, like Eve, and wants them to live quietly in a domestic setting. He is certainly not ruling out the possibility that they can be saved if they continue in faith, love, holiness and modesty. We know from other sources that Ephesus, with its cult of the goddess Artemis or Diana, was a hotbed of female assertiveness and immorality. Her temple boasted scores of sacred prostitutes – union with one of them gave you access to the goddess. But it is more than likely that these women to whom Paul refers were of high social standing. They would have had authority over the slaves in their households and would expect to be obeyed. The previous verses support this view, since the women in question wear expensive clothes, gold and pearls for jewellery, and they arrange their hair in the latest fashions (1 Tim. 2.9–10). When women like this joined the

Christian community, they would have been eager to teach, and liable to domineer over the poorly educated pastors as a natural result of their cultural background. Many of these pastors would have come from humbler backgrounds than their own, since we know that early Christianity brought a great many slaves and freedmen to faith. Frankly, these women showed a lack of respect for those charged with leading the church. They might have enjoyed a good standing in society, but they were totally unschooled as far as the gospel and Scripture went.

So the apostle will not stand for it. They are not to teach and domineer. They need to learn. He gives three reasons for this, one from creation, one from the fall, and one from redemption. Woman is part of God's creation: Adam was formed first then Eve, indicating the inclusiveness of Eve in the human race, and so she is not to be excluded from learning. She fell through deception, and as truth is the only answer to deception, she needs to learn. And she is included in redemption (see Gen. 3.15 where the Saviour is described as the seed of the woman) and therefore is no longer judged as a transgressor but is allowed to learn. Let these latter-day daughters of Eve *learn*, get clear about salvation, and adopt the role assigned to Eve of home, family, love and holiness. Paul's emphasis on the woman's role in childbearing may be a shaft at the false teachers who had disparaging views about sex and marriage (1 Tim. 4.3) and whose later Gnostic successors according the Irenaeus (*Adversus Haereses* 1.24.2) declared that 'marriage and the begetting of children are of Satan'. My conclusion is that this prohibition of women teaching and domineering over men is due to the situation at Ephesus which Timothy has to handle.

However the whole situation may be more even complex at Ephesus where sexual licence was very prevalent. A fascinating piece of research has been done in recent years by K. Kroeger and others over the meaning of *authentein*, normally translated 'exercise authority over' in verse 12. It occurs nowhere else in the New Testament. It is clearly a crucial word in this passage, however, and this passage plays a key role in the argument that a woman should never teach in mixed company, and thus exercise authority over men. Paul must have had a reason for using this rare word – he uses the normal Greek word for 'having authority over' in 1 Corinthians 7.4, *exousiazo*. The background of the word *authentein* in secular Greek writers like Euripides, Phrynicus and Philodemus is erotic. It is used of prostitutes enticing men to spend time with them. The same is true of its use in Wisdom 12.6. The word has strong sexual overtones, and Chrysostom is probably right in understanding it in his *Commentary* here on 1 Timothy to mean 'sexual licence'.

This, of course, utterly alters the meaning of the passage. Paul is saying that he does not allow a woman to teach men obscenity and fornication. This was a serious problem in the ancient Church, with all the female-based fertility cults which came over from paganism. The Thyatiran Jezebel taught Christians to practise immorality (Rev. 2.20, cf. Num. 25.1–3; 31.15f., and see 2 Peter 2.14f., together with 2 Tim. 3.6f.). Licentious doctrine and practice played an enormous part in some of the Gnostic movements which were even then beginning to invade the Church. Clement of Alexandria, in the second century, complains of those who turn the love feasts into orgies, and significantly he uses the very same word, *authentes* (*Stromata*, 3.18).

This interpretation would make excellent sense of the whole passage. Women are urged to dress modestly in a city where there are many courtesans. 'Silence' would indicate learning Christian doctrine quietly – the Greek word does not necessarily mean 'saying nothing'. In Ephesus, where many sacred prostitutes were attached to the shrine of Artemis, worshippers were taught that sex with them brought you into close union with the deity. But Christian converts must learn that there is only one God and only one mediator between God and man, the man Christ Jesus (2.5). They must practise their faith in quiet decorum, not with the obscenities entailed in Ephesian religion. Moreover, the devil had once deceived Eve (the verb 'deceive' in 2.14 probably also has sexual overtones). And to women who may have been involved in the immoralities of one of the cults the admonition Paul gives is highly appropriate. Most of the women who had the liberty to circulate freely and teach in Greek society were *hetairai,* wealthy courtesans, and doubtless they made it evident in the course of their lectures that they would be available afterwards. But the book of Proverbs had made it plain that to seduce a man in this way was to lead him to slaughter (Prov. 5.1–6; 7.6–27); and 'murder' is the other ancient connotation of the word *authentein.* In this rare word the erotic and the destructive combine. So what Paul is doing here is warning against women who lead men to spiritual death through their enticing obscenities.

I do not know that this interpretation of a difficult passage can be proved. But it makes sense. It does justice to the Greek, to the whole context, to the thought of Paul, to the power of the gospel and to the meretricious background of Ephesus. It has the further attraction of removing the glaring inconsistency from an apostle who clearly did use women in ministry and yet in this passage appears to deny them any lot or part in it. If this interpretation is even a serious possibility – and it is – it ought to loosen up a great many of the restrictive attitudes on the subject which are surprisingly still found among Christians who genuinely want to find out what the Bible teaches and be guided by it. It seems to me illegitimate to exclude half of humankind from up-front ministry, largely on the grounds of a single rare word which can be taken in several different ways! At all events it should make us think again, and perhaps ensure that Christianity which was in the van of women's liberation in the first century, is not one of the last bodies in the twenty-first century to allow women a significant place in leadership.

But there is more to be said. There is a difference between ministry and leadership. There are many ministries in the Church and God gives aptitudes for them to his people without regard to gender, race or anything else. The wise church is one which allows its members, men, women and children, the freedom to exercise the ministries God has given them. And for far too long, many branches of the Church have precluded women from preaching and sacramental functions. This has wronged and diminished women. As far as leadership is concerned, the Church has been sharply divided in recent decades. There are some Anglo-Catholics, Evangelicals, and Independent church leaders who are firmly opposed to female leadership, albeit for different reasons. On the other hand there has been a strong cry for women's leadership, fuelled partly by feminism in society and partly from a re-examination of the biblical texts. However, there are problems in the current scene, and they do not only concern the issue of women bishops. The Church as an institution is seen by many as feminine. Two-thirds of its members, at least in the UK, are female. And the ordination nowadays of rather more women than men to its clergy underlines that perception of the Church as feminine and makes it less than attractive to men.

So I wonder if there is a third possibility. When you look down history in every culture across the world, men have tended to take the role of leadership. In the Bible, it is just the same. There are the exceptions we have looked at, but the overall picture is clear, and it is male. Is this a hang-up of patriarchal society, or is there something in it for us to learn from? 'Leadership is male' wrote David Pawson. As we have seen, that is an overstatement. But would it be fair to suggest that leadership is normally male? However, should not room be made for women in leadership roles whenever it is plain that God has gifted them for it, when, for example, a Margaret Thatcher-like figure emerges? But the best leadership (and this is very much a New Testament model) is shared between men and women working together in a team, like Aquila and Priscilla, whether or not the 'head', the servant leader of such a team, is a woman or a man.

8

Paul on leadership

————————

The Pastoral Epistles give us a good, if tantalizing, insight into church leadership towards the end of the apostle Paul's life. They span the period between the rather shadowy *proistamenoi* (1 Thess. 5.12; Rom. 12.8), 'people giving the lead', of his earlier epistles and the full-blown monarchical episcopacy which we find at the end of the century with Ignatius of Antioch. These letters show how Christian leadership was developing, and something of the background against which it was taking shape.

The most notable feature is the place of Timothy and Titus, trusted colleagues of the apostle Paul and clearly operating as *ad hoc* apostolic delegates, who are charged with setting up leaders in Ephesus and Crete respectively. Although the two centres are different, and the situation in Crete is much less advanced than in Ephesus, the background, the qualities in leaders, and the purpose they serve have a lot in common. They certainly have a good deal to teach us today.

The background

The background worried Paul a great deal. It was not just that there were false teachers around, but that they came from within the core of the Christian community itself, unlike their counterparts addressed in the letters to Galatia and Corinth where they seem to have mainly come from outside. These were Christian leaders: they were teachers (1 Tim. 1.3, 7; 6.3) and teaching was the task of the *presbuteroi*, the elders. It is clear that these troublesome teachers had found a fruitful field among some women, particularly younger widows who had opened their homes to them and helped spread their teachings (1 Tim. 2.9–15; 5.11–15). And because Ephesus did not have one single church but was a fairly large Christian community, composed of a number of house churches, there was the danger that entire house churches could be led astray.

The nature of their teaching is not entirely clear. But it certainly involved both lifestyle and doctrine. The descriptions in 1 Timothy 1.3–7; 4.1–5; 6.3–10, show that they were not only arguing over words and speculations, but were proud, divisive and greedy. They were particularly avaricious for money. Their teaching was in some way related to the Old Testament, with emphasis on asceticism, food regulations, debates about the law, and wearisome genealogies. Syncretism was in the air, and both Hellenistic Jews and Gentiles had fallen for it, with lots of emphasis on knowledge and wisdom which they claimed for themselves, in contrast to the ordinary Christians to whom they felt superior. Not so very different from what Paul had to deal with in Corinth and Colossae. The church needed to hear that these deviations were a disease, and that what Timothy would teach would be 'sound' or 'healthy' doctrine. Paul urges him repeatedly to 'guard the deposit' 'fight the noble fight' 'proclaim the message' 'give attention to the public reading of scripture' because 'all scripture is inspired by God'.

Titus, like Timothy, is the apostle's delegate, left in Crete to 'straighten out what was left unfinished', particularly the appointing of elders in the various churches of the island (1.5) and sorting out the opposition and strange teachings that were troubling the Christian community. Their instigators belong to the circumcision group; they are eloquent, deceptive, they peddle Jewish myths and deliberately reject the truths of the gospel. They claim to know God, but their actions prove that they do not. So much emerges from Titus 1.10–16. A little more detail emerges in 3.9ff. These people are quarrelsome and divisive, and are always engaged in unprofitable debates about the law. But the apostle seems less urgent in this letter than in 1 Timothy. He focuses less on the false teachers and more on the people of God, called to attract others to the faith through their good works.

All of this added up to a troublesome situation for the young Christian communities. Some of their members had come from Judaism with its varied strands of emphasis on law-keeping and circumcision on the one hand, and fanciful speculation on the other. Some of them came from a variety of Gentile backgrounds with a good deal of religious baggage that was inimical to the gospel, and a lifestyle that was often scandalous. It was a difficult task for Timothy and Titus to handle, and it is not surprising that the apostle was concerned and wrote in such forthright terms.

There are obvious similarities with the present day. Ambition for money or position, divisiveness, lax morals, argumentativeness about secondary issues, teachings impossible to reconcile with the gospel, all disfigure the Christian scene. There are church leaders today who are advocating free love, homosexual marriage, rejection of the teaching of the Bible and profitless speculations. There are clergy who do not believe in God, do not believe Jesus is divine, and regard atonement as unnecessary on the ground that if God exists he accepts everyone and every lifestyle without the need for change. Scripture is not normative for them. They see the Bible as just a collection of primitive ideas about God: in any case the Church wrote the Bible and the Church can change its teachings. I have worked in the USA and have personally heard all of these positions advocated by priests and bishops in the Episcopal Church,

USA. So the warnings of the Pastoral Epistles are by no means out of date.

The qualities needed in Christian leaders

Both Timothy and Titus are urged by the apostle to identify potential leaders. This is an important aspect of leadership. The prohibition against recent converts and the need for a good reputation are obvious qualities, along with special abilities suitable for leadership such as shepherding, teaching, rebuking and offering hospitality. But none of this will avail without character. Often this is forged in the crucible of hardship and suffering. As Paul remarked, 'we also rejoice in our sufferings, because we know that suffering produces perseverance; perseverance, character; and character, hope' (Rom. 5.3). Joseph and Moses, two of the most outstanding Old Testament leaders, spent years of preparation in hard times and obscurity, and conditions will certainly have been no easier for members of a despised sect at the bottom of Roman society in the first century. So what qualities are Timothy and Titus to look for in potential leaders?

The first thing to notice in the list of qualities the apostle looks for in his letters both to Timothy (1 Tim. 3.1ff.) and Titus (1.5ff.) is that the leadership of the local churches is plural. 'Elders' and 'overseers' are synonymous in the Pastoral Epistles just as they are in Acts 20.17 and 28. It is probable that the term 'elders' covers both overseers and deacons. Plurality in leadership is a wise precaution against exaggerated egos! Their role is not spelt out in detail but included both teaching and caring for the local church. And as Paul reminds Timothy (1 Tim. 3.1) it is a noble task – the health of the churches is dependent to a large extent on their leadership. The lives of the leaders must reinforce, not contradict, their message. The leaders, Paul insists, must be above reproach. In the verses that follow, he spells out what he means in a number of ways.

First, the leader's *sex life*. He must be literally 'a one-woman man'. In a job where there will be numerous young women in his congregation, there must be no suspicion of promiscuity; his conduct must not give rise to ugly rumours. Time after time during my ministry I have seen promising clergy destroyed by sexual failure.

His *family life* must be a commendation for the gospel. He needs to be able to give a good example to his family and have his children well brought up. After all, as Paul comments, if a man does not know how to manage his own household, how can he take care of God's Church? This is one of the most demanding requirements for ministers of the gospel. They love their job and they love their family. And it is all too easy to get the balance of time and commitment wrong. 'If anyone does not provide for his relatives, and especially for his immediate family, he has denied the faith and is worse than an unbeliever' is the wise bachelor Paul's blunt advice to married pastors and others (1 Tim. 5.8). If we let the job squeeze out the family we have lost everything. Sometimes, sadly, the children reject the Christian faith because they feel it has robbed them of their dad. This is a regular problem in clergy families, and it is essential to avoid it.

His *spiritual life* next comes up for review. Wisely Paul cautions against putting a new believer, however talented, into leadership. It is all too easy for him to give way to rash judgement and pride; and pride is the primal sin. The inner life is to be nourished by prayer and the reading of Scripture, and must be given time to develop.

The elder's *personal life* is of critical importance. He must be self-controlled, not violent or liable to fly off the handle in a difficult committee meeting – that is one of the fastest ways to ruin a reputation. He must not be a drunkard, or even 'given to much wine'. Drink is addictive, dulls the perception and lends itself to ugly rumours. He must not be a lover of money; never must it appear that a Christian leader is in the job for the sake of monetary reward.

His *relationships* are extremely important. He must not be quarrelsome but a man of peace. He must not be abrupt with people, but gentle. He must care for widows. He must not hide away in his study, but be hospitable. After all, God has been hospitable to us, welcoming us into his household. Christian leaders need to model that same hospitality to others.

His *public life* needs to be dignified. It is important that he is well thought of by non-Christians.

His *ministerial life* needs to have at least two noticeable qualities. He needs to be *didaktikos* as 1 Timothy 3.2 and 2 Timothy 2.24 have it, 'able to teach'. 'He must hold firmly to the trustworthy message, as it has been taught, so that he can encourage others by sound doctrine and refute those who oppose it' (Titus 1.9). It is evident from these Pastoral Epistles that the ability to teach the faith attractively, and in a way consistent with the life of Christ and the Old Testament Scriptures, was a vital ingredient in the elder's work. It still is. If a vicar is hopeless as a teacher people will not want to listen and may well leave the church. Then he himself will become discouraged and lose heart. In the qualities set out for elders in these two letters, the ability to teach is the only quality which is not a moral or ethical one. It is clearly vital.

But if the positive teaching of the faith is one side of the coin, the other consists in the rejection of error. In all three Pastoral Epistles this is part of the role of the elder, just as it was in Ephesus years earlier when Paul warned his young leaders that false teachers would be likely to arise among them, and must be resisted. But addressing error is something we do not like to do. We prefer these days to follow the flow of secular opinion, not to go out on a limb by opposing it. For instance, everyone knows that the Roman Catholics and the Evangelicals are against abortion. But much of the rest of the Church accepts it. Equally, it is the Roman Catholics and Evangelicals, both strong on biblical content, that stand up for marriage as the only proper context for sex, while much of the rest of the Church quietly settles for fornication, adultery, homosexual intercourse and same-sex marriage as being quite acceptable. There is of course a right and a wrong way to make our stand, but these letters make it plain that the repudiation of actions which are essentially destructive of human well-being is part of the role of Christian leaders. This holds good within the Christian community as well. 'Rebuking can be one of the hardest things to learn, though it is essential for leaders', writes Dr Justyn Terry in his *Five Phases of Christian Leadership*. 'This skill is best learned from others who are more experienced, or from professional training in how to have such a delicate conversation.' There are few areas where a combination of tact and honesty are more needed.

And there is a final requirement for Christian leaders: to do their best to maintain unity in the Church. This may not always be possible, but it should be a goal. The very last injunction of Paul to Titus is that after a warning, he should have nothing to do with anyone who causes divisions, for these devastate the body of Christ (3.10–11). Sometimes division happens through the fault of the minister, perhaps by emphasizing one aspect of the Christian faith to the neglect of others, or by having a row with a feisty member of the congregation. Sometimes it happens through a breakdown of relations, between vicar and curate, vicar and organist. In the Episcopal Church of the USA, where I worked for some years, division has happened on a massive scale because of the official adoption of unbiblical doctrine and ethics, combined with ruthless lawsuits against church leaders and congregations which opposed it. But however it happens, it is always sad when the body of Christ, called to unity, gets fragmented. It must break the heart of the Jesus who prayed on the night before his death that his followers might be one, just as he and the Father were one, with the result that people would come to faith (John 17.20–24). Christian disunity certainly calls down scorn from critics, and rightly so. If we cannot agree among ourselves, why should others join us?

The dangers for Christian leaders

As Paul surveys the lifestyle of the false teachers, and urges a different way of life on the elders Timothy and Titus are called to ordain, a number of dangers emerge which are prevalent today.

One danger is *getting embroiled in controversies*, often on very secondary matters. The first letter to Timothy begins with a robust warning against Timothy occupying himself with 'myths and endless genealogies. These promote controversies rather than God's work – which is by faith'. Such warnings continue throughout the letters. A brief survey of the correspondence columns in the Church press reveals that many modern ministers need to heed that warning! Think of the amount of clerical time and learning which has been devoted, for example, to discerning whether bishops are essential, advantageous or simply useful for the Church – while vast tracts of the Christian map, and often those that are growing fastest, have no bishops at all but are led by quite different ministerial patterns, and are growing vigorously! Paul would endorse the adage 'Keep the main thing the main thing.' So often we fail to do that.

Another danger is *ambition*. Some people 'want to be

teachers of the law but they do not know what they are talking about or what they so confidently affirm' (1 Tim. 1.7). There is an academic ambition among some ministers which can be a distraction; among others it is a desire to be recognized, or to climb the clerical ladder; among others it is the love of money. All varieties of ambition, apart from the ambition to be the best for God, are dangerously at variance with the humility of Jesus Christ and his apostles. In this very chapter Paul recalls with shame and humility his previous violent, blasphemous life, and revels in the mercy of Jesus who 'came into the world to save sinners – of whom I am the foremost'. We need, like Paul, to return frequently to the cross, realize what we once were, and what it cost the Lord to rescue us. That should keep us humble.

Legalism was a danger then, and it still is. It may come through failing to understand that the purpose of law was to restrain evil, not to put a yoke round the neck of believers (1 Tim. 1.8ff.). Or it may come by imposing restrictions on the legitimate use of conscience – Paul mentions abstaining from food in 4.3. Christianity is not a system of narrow regulation. God created these things. They are to be received with thanksgiving by believers who know the truth. For everything created by God is good and nothing is to be rejected 'because it is consecrated by the word of God and prayer'. As Paul earlier wrote to the Galatians, 'for freedom Christ has set us free', and we should not allow ourselves to be brought under a yoke of legalistic bondage again, the man-made list of do's and don'ts.

Prayer is often underlined in these letters, particularly 'I urge, then, first of all, that requests, prayers, intercession and thanksgiving be made for everyone' (1 Tim. 2.1). Curiously enough, earnest believing prayer often tends to drop out of the life of many Christian leaders. We would never admit it, of course, but reliance on God in prayer gets eclipsed by reliance on the religious system we have set up, reliance on our technology, or sheer activism. We forget or explain away Jesus' words: 'Apart from me you can do nothing.' We unconsciously assume that without him we can achieve quite a lot. And so prayerlessness ensues, particularly in the West. The developing world, having far less of the material goods and technical toys of the West, is generally much more prone to pray. They know that if they do not pray they will indeed have nothing. It is a very salutary lesson for any leader. One survey revealed that many ordinary Christians tend to pray for a minute a day, and ministers for two minutes. I caught myself failing in this very area as I wrote this paragraph. My computer flashed up the invitation to lead a university mission, and I am ashamed to say that my first move was not to pray but to look in my diary to see if I could manage the dates!

Another danger for leaders is to *misuse and misinterpret Scripture*. 'Do your best', says Paul to Timothy, 'to present yourself to God as one approved, a workman who does not need to be ashamed and who correctly handles the word of truth.' By way of contrast Hymenaeus and Philetus have 'wandered away from the truth. They say that the resurrection has already taken place' (2 Tim. 2.15ff.). While the precise nature of what they taught is debated, they were clearly twisting Scripture to fit in with their own presuppositions. No wonder Paul adds 'they destroy the faith of some'. A lot of ministers do not really believe in the inspiration of Scripture. They see it as a collection of early Christian reflections. I was for some years a member of the Church of England's Doctrinal Commission. The mishandling of biblical material within the Commission led me to ask if I could present a paper 'Towards the possibility of revelation'. This I did, and I found myself in a very small minority! It is not surprising that those who do not believe in revelation often play fast and loose with Scripture. But when you do believe that God has worked through and with human authors to produce what we call Scripture, then it is important to immerse yourself in it, assess its background, and understand its thrust if you are going to faithfully interpret it to your congregation, rather than simply regale them with your own ideas, or those of current theologians.

A further danger for Christian leaders is that there is rarely a check on their *accountability*. Their work is largely unsupervised. They can operate to a large extent as they think best. And congregations are rarely in the position to hold them to account. In theory episcopal churches should be good at this. They have, after all, a bishop to supervise. But he is a busy man and is usually in charge of more than a hundred congregations. A problem will not come his way unless it has become acute. So the average minister can make the mistake of working all hours of the day and night to the neglect of health and family. Or he can be lazy, reluctant to visit, train, or prepare properly: six days invisible and one day incomprehensible! The Christian churches need to develop a much stronger accountability structure for their leaders.

A final danger worth mentioning is a form of *asceticism* which in Ephesus involved the renunciation of marriage and abstinence from certain kinds of food, and possibly wine (cf. 1 Tim. 4.3; 5.23). Since Paul goes out of his way to emphasize the goodness of all God's creation (1 Tim. 4.3–5) it seems that those he criticizes disparaged the material order. Their spiritualizing of the resurrection would fit with this worldview and so would their claim to a higher, esoteric *gnosis*, 'knowledge' (1 Tim. 6.20). These, together with a fascination for genealogies, are all hints of the later Gnosticism which proved such a danger to the early Church. It is not dead today. There are plenty of ministers who lay claim to a higher type of knowledge than lay people in their congregations. There are some who see asceticism and rigid rules as the means of earning God's favour. There are many who spiritualize the bodily resurrection of Jesus. But authentic Christianity will have none of this. This world and everything in it is the product of the good Creator God. Our bodies are of great importance to him, capable of being temples of the Holy Spirit. And the ultimate destiny of humankind is not some ethereal and bodiless heaven but a new heaven and a new earth inhabited by beings who have resurrection bodies – of which the only example at present is the risen Christ.

The purpose of Christian leaders

As we come towards the end of this book, we could well ask ourselves the question 'What are Christian leaders for? After all, they can be arrogant, immoral, divisive, ambitious and the rest – why bother with them at all? Why not have a democracy in every church, as we do in most Western societies?' But even when we do have democracy, we find it necessary to elect leaders. And it is so in every organization. Without leadership it does not get very far. That is presumably one reason why Jesus chose 12 apostles to act as leaders in his new community. And from the very first, leadership has continued to be a mark of all the varied expressions of Christianity. These Pastoral Epistles leave us with five clear impressions about the purpose of leadership in the Christian Church.

The first is *vision*. This is implied rather than emphasized in these letters. But the apostle has a vision for the growth and well-being of the church in Ephesus and in Crete, and these three letters embody that vision very clearly. Timothy and Titus, themselves apostolic delegates, are to ordain other ministers who are to give a lead in the local churches. Vision is essential. I know well a church which in many ways is ideal: large, loving congregations, a big impact on the community, a great deal of public service, good worship, almost all headed by various lay leaders. But the vicar has been absent for more than a year and the lack of direction, of vision, is palpable. Without vision the people may not perish but they certainly do not advance with much assurance.

The second is *example*. This is urged upon both Timothy and Titus. They must 'walk the talk'. 'Good works' is a phrase that runs through the letter to Titus. Leaders must lead exemplary – Paul dares to say 'blameless' – lives. Godly example carries much more weight than godly teaching. And that is why Paul gives such prominence in these letters to the quality of lifestyle that is necessary in the leaders they ordain. You only have to think of the minister whose hand is in the church funds, or the vicar who runs off with a choirboy, to realize that the congregation will be scarred and broken for years to come.

The third quality which emerges from this study is the importance of *biblical teaching*. The belief and behaviour of true followers of Jesus often goes against the grain of contemporary society. And therefore the leaders must go deeply into the teaching of their Master, learn how to contextualize it for today's world, and then fearlessly preach it. The churches that are growing throughout the world consistently seem to be those where the teaching of the Bible is given great prominence. And for that to happen, the minister needs not only to be a student of the Bible, but to have the ability to explain and apply it first to himself (hence the importance of example) and then to his congregation. I have lived in Oxford for a good many years, and it is patently obvious that the three biblically oriented Anglican churches in the heart of the city, though despised by more 'advanced' clergy, are far and away the largest, the most dynamic and the most outward-looking.

But the teaching role which Paul so strongly enjoins upon Timothy and Titus and those they ordain is not merely to teach the truths of Scripture but to *rebuke error*. 'He must hold firmly to the trustworthy message . . . so that he can encourage others by sound doctrine and refute those who oppose it' (Titus 1.9). Most ministers do very little confuting of error. It could seem narrow-minded. It could raise a storm. It could result in unpopularity, perhaps even a lawsuit. But it is part of the calling of a leader. Of course it needs to be done lovingly, humbly and tactfully, but it still needs to be done. Many in our churches will not see the importance of truth unless they are alerted to the danger of error. Some years ago a group of quite distinguished theologians jointly produced a book called *The Myth of God Incarnate.* This was a specific attack on the central Christian belief in the divinity of Jesus Christ. Part of it was published in a Sunday paper and made a big splash. My publisher asked me to get together an equally distinguished group of theologians to defend the truths that were being attacked. The book, entitled *The Truth of God Incarnate*, was written with great speed and urgency and launched in Church House Westminster to a bevy of journalists, religious and secular. It was a public rebuttal of the erroneous teaching; it sold five times as many copies as the original book; and it was a courteous but firm example of rejecting error. I invited one of the *Myth* contributors to come to our church at St Aldate's, Oxford, and put his point to our large morning congregation for 20 minutes and I would then reply for 20 minutes. This, of course, packed the place out, and he was very nervous, making sure that we did not say the creed! Nor did he make an impressive case. But the public debate over an issue of false doctrine proved very cathartic.

Not only is the minister called to teach and rebuke, but *encouragement* is one of the most important parts of his calling. Most of us struggle along spiritually, grasping at whatever help is available. In many churches there is not a lot of encouragement. There are appeals for money, standards to achieve, services to attend, jobs that need doing – but not a lot of encouragement, either for the congregation as a whole, or for individuals, who often feel that they do not really count, and are being taken for granted. Happy the leader who makes encouragement a major part of his or her ministry. The church comes alive. The congregations remains united. Sacrifices are made not because of duty but out of love and gratitude. And ordinary members of the congregation feel they are loved and appreciated – and that puts a spring in their step.

Such were some of the concluding insights of the apostle Paul towards the end of his life. And those insight are highly relevant two thousand years later. Ministry that is shared, exemplary, loving, Bible-based, fearless, visionary and encouraging will see the Christian Church flourish, whatever the social and political situation.

9

Lessons for today

Looking back over the material we have surveyed, it is remarkable that there is such unanimity in the picture they paint of early Christian ministry. This is all the more astonishing when you recall that some of this material comes from a Galilean fisherman, some from an educated rabbi, some from a Gentile doctor, and some from Jesus himself.

None of them seems to be concerned with a single exclusive model of leadership such as episcopal, congregational or presbyterian government. None of them envisages an extended period of study that is not related to the proclamation of the gospel. None of them recommends one-person leadership. None of them exalts performance over lifestyle.

On the other hand they all agree in laying enormous emphasis on character: issues like drink, sexual conduct, handling money, the willingness to suffer for the faith are paramount. They emphasize the importance of vision in leadership, and keeping the focus of that vision on Jesus Christ rather than on secondary matters.

They are strong on the biblical basis of the message, the need for courageous preaching and unmasking error, together with encouragement and the care for the vulnerable and the preservation of unity. They all lay great emphasis on practical training. They were unwilling to compromise in order to accommodate the prevalent political correctness. Indeed their oft-repeated claim that Jesus is Lord was not primarily a religious but a political manifesto. It claimed that Jesus, not Caesar, was supreme in the universe, and that, of course, could be – and often was – viewed as treason and the justification for persecution. They knew they were a counter-culture and they were prepared to go to prison, and if need be to death, for their convictions.

How does our understanding of leadership compare with these first-century convictions? In many ways we share them. We know that character is important. We take considerable care over selection. We give training in theology, the biblical languages, ethics and perhaps some philosophy. But there are whole areas on which they concentrated where we are weak. Here are a few of them.

First and foremost, as we have seen, our training of Christian leaders is normally conducted in a college, for two or three years, with the main emphasis on academic achievement rather than intentional preparation for active ministry. The students of today are going to be involved tomorrow in evangelism, apologetics, and the running of a church, which is like a small business. Very few colleges give any instruction or practice in evangelism. Very few take the trouble to find out the main objections to Christianity in the culture and train students to handle them effectively. And there is, so far as I am aware, no training in the management of people and the running of an organization. Most clergy and ministers are singularly weak in all three areas, and this can be traced back to their training.

Few of our regular Christian leaders are trained on the job, and that is where we are at a disadvantage compared with other professionals. As we noted, accountants, nurses, doctors, teachers are not trained primarily in academic institutions, though they make use of them. The accountancy students get out and do actual accounting with real customers quite early in their training. You will find the young nurses and doctors on the wards, the trainee teachers in the classroom. Of course they will be under supervision, just as the young leaders were in New Testament times. But the emphasis has to be on training for a specific purpose, into which they are introduced early in their training. This then becomes formative for their development. As we saw, St Mellitus College does precisely that: hence its great appeal. People are quick to see the relevance of its training methods.

As you read this, you may yourself be undergoing training in a seminary of the traditional type, and you may be wondering how to cope. My advice from many years of experience would be this. Do your academic work with diligence. Seek to be the best you can. Read widely in the area of Christian apologetics. Seek to prepare yourself not merely for examinations but for future ministry. You will never in later life have the opportunity for such extended study. But ensure that you have some regular ministry outlet. The nature of the outlet is not important. But to have some regular avenue of practical service for the Lord saves you from being enmeshed in the theological college bubble, and balances the large amount of academic information that you naturally have to take on board.

A second emphasis which marked the first Christians is this. They trained their leaders to make Jesus Christ Lord of their whole lives. They inculcated a vision to serve him by bringing others to faith and creating communities of love and sacrifice which stood out in striking contrast to general conditions in the Roman Empire. We share their vision of including the poor, the ill-educated, those from a variety of races, and this is admirable. The Church is always meant to be both a hospital and an army. As a hospital, today's Christian Church can claim much credit. But as an army, with a clear message and vision for impacting society with the good news of Jesus Christ, we must surely hang our heads in shame. We are not seen as a fascinating if dangerous counter-culture, which the early Christians were. We are seen as an irrelevance, a weak 'faith community' that is inoffensive, kindly, and good for complementing the social deficiencies of the welfare state. But we are rarely seen as a passionate community burning with a message which must be passed on as a matter of life and death.

There is another very obvious contrast. We train our ministers for sole leadership. To be sure, there are steps on the upward path – youth minister, assistant minister, senior minister in some churches – or curate, priest, bishop in others. But at the pinnacle you will almost always find one person. That is emphatically repudiated in all the leadership models that we see in the New Testament. There is always a plurality of leadership, for the excellent reasons that we have seen. My colleague at St Aldate's Oxford, the Revd David Prior, himself an outstanding leader, had two very wise maxims on this subject. One was an emphasis on 'a fellowship of leadership'. Leaders should not be alone, but like those at Antioch (Acts 13.1) should be plural. They should be a team. This goes a long way to share the load, to prevent burnout, and to offer a model of self-giving and loving partnership which in due course permeates every organization in the parish. David's other maxim was 'Nobody should minister without being ministered to.' This is another aspect of shared leadership which is very important and which is widely neglected in the pattern we encourage. Many students are told not to make close friends within their congregation or parish – for fear of appearing to have favourites. But if not, where are they going to gain support from? They are going to have to suppress their problems, and this courts danger later on. It tends to foster the myth that the leader is above the petty frailties of ordinary Christians – until the crash happens.

Another area where we could usefully learn from first-century leaders is in their commitment to Scripture. This is everywhere to be seen: in Jesus himself, in the apostles and in what they required of their young leaders. Almost every page of the New Testament shows how deeply its leaders were steeped in the Old Testament Scriptures and how they applied what they found there. Today in most colleges there is a lot of worship which includes considerable swathes of Scripture, but frequently there is little wrestling with the text in any depth learning how to expound its meaning with passion and clarity or conviction that this is God's revelation to mankind, rather than mankind's ideas about God. Although the formularies of most denominations accord a supreme place to Scripture, this is by no means always the case with many of the actual leaders within those denominations, or the students they send out Indeed, so confused is the Christian message, so unsure about its ultimate authority, that most people have no idea what the Church is supposed to stand for on any contentious issue.

It is rash to generalize, but in New Testament days they seemed to place greater emphasis on the character and lifestyle of those they allowed into leadership than we do, particularly in the areas of sexuality, the love of money, ambition, the importance of relationships, and the need for courage in the face of hardship. What, however, is beyond dispute is that we need to learn from their insistence on the leader being able to teach well and to give the lead. Many of our clergy could hardly be described as leaders. They are operatives who keep the church going in its accustomed ways. They are into main- tenance, not mission. They have not been trained in evangelism or the building up of new believers. They have not been trained in leading inductive Bible studies without dominating them They have not been trained to proclaim the gospel powerfully and attractively in the different settings of a church, a pub, a restaurant meeting, or the open air. And they certainly have not been trained to withstand error in a clear but gracious manner

There is one other area where the contrast, at least between the Church in the West and the primitive Church, is so noteworthy. Most of us today do not pay much more than lip service to the work of the Holy Spirit. This is a very serious weakness when you reflect that it is the Spirit who convicts people of their need, the Spirit who makes Jesus attractive to them, and the Spirit who enables them to cry 'Jesus is Lord' and experience the new birth. This pre-eminence of the Spirit continues in the fruit of holy living and in the special gifts he longs to shower upon Christians. But because many of our churches pay little attention to the Spirit, two consequences ensue. The quality of Christian character remains unimpressive and not very different from the lifestyle of those who are not Christians. Also there is not much reliance on the power of the Spirit to guide, to convict and convert, let alone to heal, to exorcize and to prophesy. Is this not an area of leadership where we have much to learn from the New Testament leaders?

For all these reasons, I believe we will profit by looking back to the first Christian leaders. They are the magnetic north, so to speak, by which we can set our often volatile compass. They could help us, two thousand years later, to cut a more distinctive and effective furrow in our society, which is as godless today as theirs was, but where our current Christian Church, at least in the West, makes far less impact. What passes for Christian leadership has often down the centuries been marked by egotism, ambition, cruelty and selfishness. But we have seen that these are terrible distortions of the pattern Jesus embodied and left us. As Amy Orr-Ewing, Director of the Oxford Centre for Christian Apologetics puts it, 'Christian leadership should never be about ourselves. It is ultimately focused on a purpose that is larger and wider than individual ambition, because it seeks God's kingdom coming on earth.' That is indeed the goal of radical leadership.

Printed in Great Britain
by Amazon

46989726R00071